LOWE'S
Home Improvement Warehouse
complete kitchen
BOOK

welcome home

WE AT LOWE'S SEE HOMEOWNERS COME THROUGH OUR DOORS EVERY WEEK, scratch pads and magazine clippings in hand, looking both eager and puzzled, and bent on gaining information. They want to remodel their kitchen, but the prospect can seem daunting. For good reason—a kitchen is not only a sizable financial investment, but a decidedly emotional one as well. No room of the house is as complex in its requirements, yet no room can contribute more to the harmonious functioning of a household. With all the demands on the kitchen today, a remodel needs to be done well.

This book can help.

Lowe's Complete Kitchen Book is our fourth in a series, following **Complete Home Improvement**, **Complete Landscaping**, and **Complete Home Decorating**. These books are part of our commitment to provide everything you need—ideas, advice, techniques, and tips as well as tools and materials—for projects around your home. With this book, we tackle remodeling your kitchen, from planning, decision making, and purchasing to step-by-step instructions for all kinds of projects you can do yourself.

Throughout this process, you can lean on Lowe's. Our professionals are ready to provide advice and to help you choose from the very best selection of lumber, tools, materials, appliances, and everything else you may need. Take advantage of one of our store-sponsored do-it-yourself clinics in your area, or check out the How-To Library at www.lowes.com.

Lowe's has been helping people create beautiful homes for more than five decades. We're proud to be part of making your kitchen all you want it to be.

Lowe's Companies, Inc.

Bob Tillman
CHAIRMAN/CEO/PRESIDENT

Melissa S. Birdsong
DIRECTOR, TREND
FORECASTING & DESIGN

Robin Gelly
MERCHANDISER

Bob Gfeller
SENIOR VP, MARKETING

Jean Melton
VP, MERCHANDISING

Mike Menser
SENIOR VP, GENERAL
MERCHANDISE MANAGER

Gregg Plott
DIRECTOR, MARKETING

Dale Pond
EXECUTIVE VP, MERCHANDISING

Ann Serafin
MERCHANDISE MANAGER

table of contents

Lowe's Series

PROJECT COORDINATOR René Klein

SENIOR EDITOR Sally Smith

Staff for Lowe's Complete Kitchen Book

EDITOR Don Vandervort, Hometips

MANAGING EDITOR Louise Damberg

ART DIRECTOR Dan Nadeau

TEXT & RESEARCH Steve Cory, Carol A. Crotta, Patricia Freeman, Rick Peters, Shelley Ring Diamond

ILLUSTRATION Theresa Jacobson and Dan Marks/Troxtel Design

PHOTO RESEARCH Lauren Campedelli

PRODUCTION COORDINATOR Eligio Hernandez

PROOFREADER Amy Spitalnick

EDITORIAL ASSISTANTS Gabe Vandervort, Kit Vandervort

INDEXER Rick Hurd

PRODUCTION DIRECTOR Lori Day

DIGITAL PRODUCTION Jennifer McMillen/Color Control, Jeff Curtis/Leisure Arts

On the cover

TOP LEFT: Photography: Brian Vanden Brink. Architect: Thom Rouselle. TOP RIGHT: Photography: James Frederick Housel. Architect: J. Stephen Peterson & Associates. MIDDLE: Photography: Brian Vanden Brink. Architect: Mike Homer. BOTTOM LEFT: Photography: David Wakely. Architect: Kevin Patrick O'Brien; Interior Design: Janice Stone Thomas. BOTTOM RIGHT: Photography: E. Andrew McKinney. Design: David & Vicki Ritter. Builder: David Ritter Construction

COVER DESIGN Vasken Guiragossian

10 9 8 7 6 5 4 3 2 1

First printing September 2002

Copyright © 2002

Sunset Publishing Corporation, Menlo Park, CA 94025.

ISBN 0-376-00914-4

Library of Congress Control Number: 2002110943

Printed in the United States.

recipe for success

CHANCES ARE, IF YOU ARE READING this book, you are exploring remodeling your kitchen or perhaps even designing a brand-new one. You may simply be looking for ideas, a bit of inspiration. Or you might already have a mental picture of your perfect kitchen but need some help sorting through the vast variety of kitchen-related product available today. Perhaps you simply need guidance in the actual planning, from creating a budget to hiring professionals. Or maybe you bring building skills to the table and are looking for some step-by-step instructions to do much of the work yourself.

A gallery of stunning, idea-filled kitchens will guide you through every step of planning and designing your ideal kitchen.

In any and all of these instances, you've come to the right place. Here's a preview of what's in the pages ahead:

your **ideal** kitchen

A visual guide to kitchen remodeling, from big picture to small details, this section begins with the broader concepts— getting the right kitchen for your needs, figuring out your personal style—then goes on to space and layout considerations; organization options; types of kitchens; solving space, flow, and light problems; creating an efficient kitchen; and finally, the decorative details that can tie your design together visually. Also included are sections on eye-catching budget makeovers and major remodels.

buyer's guide

This concise guide is designed to help you make informed buying choices. Kitchen elements covered here include cabinets, storage accessories and hardware, countertops, flooring options, paint and wallpaper, sinks, faucets, dishwashers, undersink fixtures, refrigerators, cooking appliances, lighting, windows and skylights, and window treatments.

project **workbook**

When you reach the planning stages of your project, this section will walk you through the many important considerations that accompany remodeling. Whether you plan to do none, some, or all of the work, this section will help you develop your

In the Buyer's Guide, you'll find more than 100 photographs of products available at Lowe's, along with invaluable decision-making information.

LOWE'S QUICK TIP

Tip boxes in the margins offer helpful ideas and time-saving tips.

Each project presented in the Do-It-Yourself Guide offers illustrated step-by-step instructions.

plan, hire and manage professionals, access Lowe's installation services, and work with contracts, codes, permits, and zoning issues.

do-it-yourself guide

For those who choose to do the work themselves, this section presents illustrated step-by-step instructions for the most common kitchen remodeling jobs. The projects presented include opening up a wall; building a simple wall; hanging, finishing and patching drywall; installing interior trim; various plumbing and electrical tasks; and installing and improving different types of flooring, cabinets, and countertops. Also

included is a guide to the tools and materials you'll need to get going.

As you make your way through the book, you'll be aided by a number of graphic presentations, as shown here. Floor plans are included where they are helpful to illustrate a concept, as are cautionary messages for do-it-yourselfers and clear step-by-step instructions for each building project. Throughout, you'll be treated to Lowe's Quick Tips, those small margin boxes, as shown above right, that offer nuggets of advice for streamlining your remodel.

So go ahead and start exploring. We'll help you through every step of the way.

a special place

CONSIDER THE KITCHEN. IT IS ULTIMATELY UTILITARIAN AND YET IMMENSELY more than just a place for preparing food. The kitchen is a place of warmth, familial closeness, and security.

It is no wonder that this room is repeatedly referred to as "the heart of the home." In simpler times, the kitchen was the home; it blended seamlessly with eating and sitting areas to serve as the core of the colonial "keeping room"—the family's living space. Over the centuries, the kitchen has retained this venerable role and, though it has become so much more, it hasn't given up the intrinsic values embodied by the humble cast-iron stewpot set over an open flame in that central room.

Despite this heritage, no other room in the American home has evolved so remarkably. In an upward spiral, technological advances have made it a far easier place in which to accomplish basic kitchen chores faster, more efficiently, and with better results. Thousands of outstanding home products, from drop-dead-gorgeous cabinets, counters, and floors to incredibly efficient appliances, have made the kitchen a work of beauty—and science.

And kitchens have expanded their role. Today's kitchens have become entertainment centers, media rooms, dining rooms, and home offices. Though life spins ever faster, with family members often occupying separate orbits, the kitchen has come to exert a kind of domestic gravity, pulling us together in an environment that is simultaneously active, comfortable, and nurturing.

For these reasons, getting a kitchen right is critically important. As you embark on your kitchen project, strive to achieve a kitchen that answers all your needs, and moreover, is the physical embodiment of the lifestyle you want for yourself and your family. This process may seem daunting at times, but, when you reach your end goal, you're sure to find it was well worth all the dreaming, scheming, and hard work.

Enjoy every minute.

your ideal kitchen

AS YOU BEGIN IMAGINING AND DESIGNING THE KITCHEN OF YOUR DREAMS, YOU may have only the broadest sense of what you want: bright and airy, warm and cozy, sleek and elegant, minimalist yet ultraefficient. It will take dozens of carefully thought-out decisions, major and minor, to turn your list of adjectives into reality. The more you've thought through the details, the easier the job will be when you find yourself face-to-face with an architect, kitchen designer, or contractor.

What makes the ideal kitchen? Efficient layout, quality appliances, clever storage—and a sunny disposition.

Over the next 64 pages, we will guide you through key kitchen-planning decisions and considerations. First, you must determine the scope of your project. This book assumes you're doing a remodel, but kitchen remakes range from a total gutting, and perhaps opening up adjacent rooms, to a modest update. You will want to think about how to integrate your new kitchen's style with your home's overall look, and what role the right materials and other design details can play in establishing that style. Other vital considerations include a kitchen's size and general layout, its connection to other areas such as a family room, and the way it is oriented to your home's lot and the view.

Your family's lifestyle is another critical factor. Do you enjoy entertaining, surrounded by guests while you cook? Does your household include two or more avid cooks who like to prepare meals together? Do you want a kitchen that's wheelchair-accessible or has universal-design features? And, finally, how can you get what you want without breaking the bank?

In addition to perusing the ideas and information on these pages, you might start keeping a scrapbook of magazine clippings, talking with friends whose kitchens you admire, and consulting with design professionals—such as the helpful people at Lowe's—for more guidance.

A great kitchen exudes warmth, enhanced here by the wood cabinetry.

Beautifully coordinated
cabinetry, range hood,
flooring, and counter-
tops achieve a seamless
blend of style and func-
tion in this design.

getting it right

WHAT MAKES A GREAT KITCHEN? A kitchen becomes great when it looks and functions just the way you want and need it to. Though there is no magic recipe for a great design, a key ingredient is knowing what does or doesn't work for your family before you start. A clear vision of the way you want to go can prevent you from being distracted along the way by the many beguiling choices.

For example, you might be dazzled by the idea of an all-white kitchen. Though a sleek white kitchen can be striking for a couple without kids, a family with young children is likely to learn that sticky handprints on pristine surfaces serve up a steady diet of headaches. Similarly, a large kitchen featuring every conceivable cooking apparatus may be a colossal waste of space and money for a single person who prefers to eat out most nights.

Layout is also critical. If you must watch over young children while working in the kitchen, an ideal scheme would allow full visibility into an adjoining family room. Similarly, if your home is located on a lot with a spectacular view, a great kitchen layout would let you enjoy the scene both while dining and while prepping and cooking.

Determining the right materials for your family's needs is also key. Pale stone countertops may work perfectly for someone able to give them the proper care, but if spilled juice is an everyday part of your life, a better choice may be one of the many solid-surface composite countertops available. And while slate or other stone flooring may look exquisite, a softer surface, such as hardwood or vinyl, will be kinder to your feet and back if you spend a lot of time cooking.

the design process

To begin, take stock of your kitchen's assets and liabilities. List its various components, including appliances, countertops, flooring, cabinetry, natural and artificial lighting, and color scheme. Indicate next to each item whether or not it's a keeper. Then make notes about how each retained element could meet your family's needs more completely.

If budget is a major issue, examine whether some of the more expensive elements are salvageable. Would refacing—

Design focal points in this modern take on the country kitchen include open shelving, a simple wrought-iron pot rack, and a fine-lined island.

rather than replacing—the cabinetry do the trick? Do you really dislike the counter tile, or would new grout give your countertops the needed facelift? Would a new coat of paint, new cabinet pulls, and new fixtures be enough to transform a drab kitchen?

Of course, some problems may demand structural solutions. A dark kitchen can brighten with larger windows, and a cramped kitchen may expand into an adjoining room or area. A new layout can eliminate poor sight lines from the kitchen to the family room. Reorienting the elements of the kitchen triangle—sink, range or stove, and refrigerator—into closer proximity with one another and adding a worktable, island, or even a second sink may do wonders to ease the kitchen workload. (For more on the kitchen triangle, see page 60.)

Analyzing what works in your kitchen and what definitely needs to be changed or improved to meet your household's needs will focus your efforts and establish your project's parameters.

Innovative cabinet detailing can turn a good kitchen design into a great one. ABOVE: "Piercing" traditional cabinetry with cutout handles and glass-panel doors lends a stylish contemporary touch. RIGHT: An unmatched assortment of knobs and pulls and reverse color fields on wall and base cabinets give simple cabinetry a witty twist.

accessible elegance Thinking beyond the box can pay off handsomely in eye-catching design. Substituting a graceful corner curve in place of the usual hard angle in this kitchen establishes a theme that carries through to the design of the curvaceous island-bar. A butcher-block countertop that unexpectedly flows upward to become the backsplash, alternating closed and open shelving, and cheery small-tile cabinet detailing are delightfully fresh touches.

what's your style?

A KITCHEN IS A WONDERFUL PLACE TO stretch your creative muscles, not just in cooking pursuits but in design and decoration. Before selecting any new colors, materials, fixtures, appliances, cabinetry, or lighting, however, you'll want to settle on an overall style.

If your home has a distinct architectural style, let that focus and inspire your design. Any period house—such as Victorian, Spanish Colonial, Arts and Crafts, or Georgian—will be enhanced by a kitchen plan that incorporates the era's design elements.

A Victorian house festooned with exuberant gingerbread trim, for example, would be utterly deflated by a sober Shaker-style kitchen. But add white glass-fronted cabinets with filigreed openwork trim, an arched-neck spigot emptying into a deep-fronted enamel sink, plus wood floors and marble countertops, and the spirit of the house comes alive. Similarly, you can enhance the rustic feel of a Spanish hacienda–style home by exposing and distressing ceilings beams, lining countertops with chunky hand-formed and brightly painted tile, and installing rough-textured cabinets.

If your house is of no specific architectural style, as is the case for most of us, you can exercise a freer hand. Nearly anything goes today—eclectic modern, simple Shaker, '50s diner, stark industrial— but the most popular styles remain traditional, contemporary, and country.

classic styles

The traditional kitchen, which adapts well to many home types, is a sedately formal style with roots in early 19th-century English design. Cabinetry, in deep-stained wood or painted cream, often features crown moldings and built-in display shelves. Countertops are fashioned from marble, granite, or their solid-surface lookalikes. Often, large utilitarian appliances such as a dishwasher and refrigerator are concealed by cabinet panels.

Taking on a decidedly darker, more masculine tone, this traditional kitchen is lightened by checkerboard flooring.

Hardware is a conspicuous design element; brass is often chosen to reinforce the period style. Lighting usually features formal hanging fixtures consistent with the overall look.

Contemporary kitchens are known for their sleek, ultraclean look—even drawer pulls and cabinet handles are minimized or removed altogether to avoid visual clutter. Contemporary materials are as sleek as the style itself: Fine-grained natural wood, chrome, stainless steel, and glass predominate. As you might imagine, countertop paraphernalia is kept to a minimum, with small appliances closeted in garages and large appliances cloaked with cabinet panels. Lighting is often recessed.

The country kitchen couldn't have a more different feel. Here, the look is casual, cozy, lived-in. Countertops may display a cheerful assemblage of baskets, canisters, and crockery. The cabinetry features plain lines with bead board, recessed or simple raised panels, often in natural or painted wood, or a combination. Windows sport cheerful curtains. Walls tend to be effusively dressed with everything from dried-flower wreaths to herb-drying racks, old plates, and antique pudding molds.

Not sure what you want? You can always hang your kitchen-decorating scheme on something as simple as a single color palette or a favorite collection of pottery. Just be true to your home's overall style.

The traditional kitchen need not be fussy. Here, expanses of modestly detailed white cabinets and a bank of simple double-hung windows create a vintage feel.

what's your style?

LEFT AND BELOW: Rustic furniture, earthy materials, and a cheerful clutter of pots, pans, and plates displayed on hanging racks and open shelving are hallmarks of the country kitchen.

ABOVE: With charming insouciance, a hand-painted meandering grapevine loosens up the studied formality of this kitchen cabinetry and gives it the country touch. RIGHT: A country kitchen celebrates its accoutrements by giving them free range, pairing them tongue-in-cheek with elegantly framed "artworks," aged silver pieces, and a formal, if distressed, mantel.

quintessential country No country kitchen is complete without a rough-hewn wood table as a centerpiece. In this case, the table does double duty as an island-bar, with storage cabinets nestled underneath. The massive exposed beams, cooktop's arched ceramic tile surround, and wood-and-tile flooring add to the country ambience, as does the clutch of baskets, pots, and pans suspended from the ceiling and hanging from the beam.

cool contemporary "The sleeker the better" is the watchword of the contemporary kitchen. Therefore, designers often use expanses of metal, polished stone, or other highly reflective surfaces, clean-lined cabinetry, and sculptural forms to make an ultramodern statement. Warming up this kitchen's cool demeanor, icy stainless-steel panels are set into traditional dark-wood cabinet framing, the two looks cleverly reconciled by elaborated metal pulls.

RIGHT: A curving elevated bar gives a view to a small kitchen of modern design anchored by a stainless-steel island, sleek hood, and angular stove-wall treatment. BELOW: Less is often more in the contemporary kitchen: Here, paraphernalia are hidden behind wall-like cabinetry, but layers of counters provide plenty of workspace for two or more cooks.

Contemporary doesn't necessarily mean stark. Bold primary-color blocks highlight this kitchen, which is "separated" from the dining area by a low perforated-metal riser on the peninsula.

small or large?

WHEN PLANNING YOUR REMODEL, determine just how big you want your kitchen to be. Though the prevailing attitude suggests that "bigger is better," a great big kitchen may not, in fact, be the right kitchen for your family. Remember, for instance, that you will pay dearly for every square foot of a new kitchen, both during construction and when maintaining, heating, and cooling the space for years to come.

ABOVE AND RIGHT: **Large kitchens offer plenty of work and storage areas, but can be exhausting to navigate without centrally located islands to break up the distances.**

When might a small kitchen make sense? If you don't really like to cook, you seldom entertain, and you lack an affinity for kitchen equipment, a compact kitchen—sink, range, refrigerator, microwave, dishwasher, and a few cabinets—would serve you just fine. Keeping the kitchen small may open up space for an office, media center, craft area, or other room that would be more useful to

you. And one of these areas will probably be far less expensive to build.

Of course, in the right circumstances, a large kitchen can be just the ticket. If your family life revolves around the kitchen, then you will want to maximize this area. You may even want to open the kitchen completely to the family room or incorporate an island-bar for casual seating. A large kitchen also makes sense if your family includes two or more cooks vying for workspace during meal preparation. If you entertain a good deal or have a lot of paraphernalia, then a large kitchen also fills the bill.

In addition, if other homes in your neighborhood have large kitchens and you are remodeling with an eye to selling your home in the near future, a large kitchen will probably help you to seal a deal faster and for more money.

Is it possible to enlarge a small kitchen without adding on? Absolutely. Identify non-load-bearing walls that can easily be removed to facilitate traffic flow and open up vistas (see pages 164–165). You might

The gleam in the eye of
this tiny U-shape kitchen
comes from its shades
of gray and generous
use of stainless steel.

A very large kitchen turns into a modern-day "keeping room," combining cooking, dining, and living areas.

even combine your kitchen, dining, and family room areas into a "great room." Consider appropriating an adjacent closet for a walk-in pantry or incorporating its square footage into the kitchen.

If you have a large kitchen that you want to make more useful, think about how its space could be better planned. The addition of a large island can gain you an eating counter, a bar, and even a stylish buffet. Or, if you want a smaller island, you might consider a movable rather than a permanent one to provide added flexibility.

Because it can be more difficult to work efficiently in a large kitchen, consider

breaking the space down into work triangles (see page 60) to save you needless steps. For example, a second sink and dishwasher near the dining room entrance might make cleanup far easier.

A large kitchen is a perfect spot for a computer station—ideally situated for you to store and retrieve recipes and catch up on e-mails while keeping an eye on that simmering pot of soup. A cook's library and a cozy telephone nook are other niceties you might consider. And if you're a gardener, adding a sink and counter by the back door would allow freshly plucked fruits and vegetables to be cleaned before being transported inside.

LEFT: Even the smallest space seems large when surrounded by window walls and a door to the garden. BELOW: With its high ceilings, sunny colors, and sophisticated detailing, this tiny kitchen has style to spare.

Bold colors, played off pale cabinets, prove that small kitchens need not be painted all white to appear spacious.

budget makeovers

IF YOUR KITCHEN NEEDS AN UPDATE but you aren't prepared for a major remodel, explore the possibilities of a budget makeover. A minor redo can yield dramatic results with a minimum of fuss and financial outlay.

Of course, a simple makeover can't improve your kitchen's layout or transform a small room into a large one, but it can camouflage all kinds of shortcomings and make the room feel bigger. Choosing a neutral, monochromatic color scheme is one way to create the illusion of more space. A dark room can be brightened with light-toned reflective paint and economical undercabinet lighting.

Because new cabinets typically account for nearly half the cost of a major kitchen remodel, one way to keep your project affordable is to clean and refurbish them, enliven them with paint, or reface them. Another option is to purchase a few new cabinets, fill in the gaps between them with open shelving, then replace the shelving with cabinetry later.

With a little ingenuity, you can remake the rest of your kitchen for very little money. Start by considering inexpensive remodeling materials, which can often be just as practical and attractive as high-priced ones. For example, you can arrange commercial vinyl tiles in a checkerboard pattern to create a striking floor. Or add panache to a budget back-

Updating this drab kitchen involved adding to-the-ceiling cabinets, a greenhouse window, and an eye-catching glass-front cabinet set in front of an existing window. Clever storage solutions include twin side-facing pullout compartments above the refrigerator for tall boxes and containers.

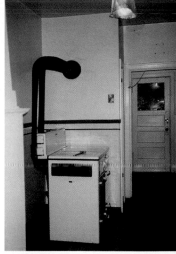

splash by laying ceramic tiles in a diagonal pattern rather than the usual grid. Search the universe of plastic laminates for textures and patterns that might make an unusual countertop.

You can even add a few upscale elements to your makeover without breaking the bank. Would you love a granite countertop? A solid stone slab can be a budget buster, but granite tiles are quite affordable. Do you have your eye on some imported ceramic tiles? Buy just a few, and use them as accent pieces. Do you wish you could afford stainless steel? Skip the costly fabrication process, and make your countertop out of flat 16-gauge stainless sheeting finished with a wood edge.

Here's an effective kitchen improvement that's free: If you have too little room for

food preparation, consider banishing your seldom-used small appliances to that cabinet above the refrigerator. Or replace them with new versions that mount under your cabinets. If your cookbook collection is taking up scarce counter space, consider building a shelf, or free up cabinet space by giving away those cracked dishes you've had since college.

A remodel doesn't have to be an all-or-nothing endeavor. You can remake your kitchen in stages: If your appliances are on their last legs, replace them first and make other changes when your bank balance recovers; if you need a new floor, put up with your old refrigerator for a while longer. The strategy is to tailor your kitchen makeover to suit your budget, your schedule, and your priorities.

Many a dated kitchen benefits from bright colors and new light sources, such as the glass door set at the end of this narrow galley kitchen. Arching the former laundry room doorway and piercing the supporting wall with columns increased the flow of light into the kitchen proper.

Small touches—open shelving, a row of decorative tiles, a whimsical wood valance, and a sunny window seat—rejuvenate a kitchen without breaking the bank.

Unless the space is being completely reconfigured, a kitchen's existing cabinets—a major expense to replace—may still work, with a bit of freshening, that is. Refacing the cabinets with new doors, capping them with decorative wood molding to the ceiling, and adding new pulls and a fresh coat of paint can be transforming.

stylish update This kitchen had good bones, which was lucky for the homeowners, who had few dollars to spend to bring it up to date. An intensely sunny yellow paint, which plays off existing cream cabinets and a dapper new black-and-white vinyl tile floor, bought at close-out price, set the tone for the punchy redesign. Removing the existing window apron visually enlarged the natural light source. New black countertops—the one splurge—are a modern touch. Broadening and extending the peninsula countertop updated the original look and created an eating counter.

major remodels

THINK ABOUT ALL THE THINGS YOU'VE ever wanted in a kitchen. Do you wish you had a sunny breakfast nook, or a spacious great room where the whole family can gather? Do you dream about custom-made cherry cabinets and granite-slab countertops? No matter what's on your wish list, a major remodel gives you the flexibility to create a kitchen that's tailor-made for you.

A full-scale redo also allows you to think big. If your kitchen is too small to accommodate the features you want, you can expand it by building an addition or moving interior walls. Converting a little-used porch or a spare bedroom into kitchen space can make room for an eating area or island. Opening the wall to an adjoining family room can give you a multipurpose area for cooking, eating, and

A major remodel often means knocking down walls or changing the ceiling. This project involved both—and the results are stunning. The addition of a peninsula not only garners critical work and storage space, but also creates a breakfast nook.

With their house newly supported by a steel beam and column, the owners replaced a solid-brick supporting wall with an eye-opening pass-through that runs the width of the kitchen proper, providing access to the dining room, formerly the sun room. The new suspended ceiling offers integrated lighting diffused through attractive wood slats.

entertaining. With square footage to spare, you can have the butler's pantry or laundry center you've always wanted. If you're a committed cook or a diehard host, enlarging your kitchen will give you all kinds of options: adding an extra workstation or a bar, installing two dishwashers, or choosing a refrigerator you like rather than settling for one that fits.

Whether or not you supersize your kitchen, you can transform it into something completely new. The list of high-impact improvements you can make is practically endless. You can change a dark, cramped space into a light, airy one by adding windows, glass doors, or skylights. If you have an attic above your kitchen, you can create a stunning effect by raising the ceiling. If your floor plan is inefficient, you can rearrange it to suit your needs. While you're at it, you can

To gain space and light, the owners doubled the size of their kitchen/ breakfast room and opened up a wall to add a window.

upgrade outdated plumbing or inadequate electrical service.

Even if your goal is simply to outfit your kitchen in style, a major remodel can really pay off. An ambitious renovation will result in a room that not only functions well but reflects your passions.

Is your style contemporary? You can set an ultramodern tone by replacing your old cabinets with sleek frameless ones. Do you adore a country cottage decor? Make a rustic center-island the focal point of your kitchen plan. Are you a serious baker? Consider a marble-topped baking center and a convection oven.

Though you may not be able to include everything you want, you can find room in the budget for the items or features you care about the most. Spring for a hardwood floor if you really want one, even though vinyl is less expensive. Splurge on the wet bar or built-in refrigerator you've long envisioned.

When it comes right down to it, even your extravagances are investments—in quality of life for you and your family. After all, the whole point of a major remodel is to create your ideal kitchen— the one that will work for you and delight you every day for years to come.

BELOW: **A glass door pulls light into the new dining area, created as part of this major remodel. Dishes are stored and displayed in a built-in china cabinet.**

STARTING FROM SCRATCH

If you are designing your kitchen from the ground up, count yourself fortunate. There's no need to peel through layers of awful remodeling attempts by previous owners, no terrible traffic patterns, poor window placement, or miserable floor plan with which to contend. You can get it right, from the start.

Kitchen planning in this circumstance begins right at the siting stage. If a kitchen or family-style "keeping room" is your priority, talk with your architect about how best to take advantage of such assets as views, favorable natural lighting, and access to the outdoors.

If you plan to live in a house a long time, and budget is a consideration, it will be worth your while to invest now in the kitchen "hardscape"—cabinets, countertops, flooring, and lighting systems—rather than blow the budget buying ultradeluxe appliances. There will be time—and hopefully savings—down the road for that $5,000 range or $8,000 refrigerator.

If you are building with the intent to sell at some point, keep in mind that a great kitchen boosts a home's value. Just take care to build within the resale values that your neighborhood can sustain.

The addition of a peninsula makes all the difference in this remodel, giving the new kitchen structure and efficiently concentrating the work area, which leaves ample room for a gracious dining "corner." Spiffy cabinetry, strong tile work, and good lighting complete the facelift.

This Craftsman-style kitchen flaunts a great view by substituting windows for walls wherever structurally possible.

light and views

ONE GOAL OF MANY KITCHEN REMODELS is to open up an otherwise dark kitchen to natural light and views. Accomplishing this isn't difficult if you're building from scratch because it's easy to situate the kitchen where it takes full advantage of your lot's assets. But, when remodeling an older home—which often has only one or two nondescript windows in the kitchen—capturing light and views can pose a challenge.

Fortunately, technological breakthroughs in window and skylight construction and design have opened up the kitchen to the outdoors in unprecedented ways. In the past, using broad expanses of glass meant severe energy loss, unwanted heat gain, and excessive glare. However, high-tech, high-efficiency glazing has all but eliminated these problems. Today, home own-

ers and designers maximize natural light by grouping sets of windows, running windows counter-to-ceiling, installing "light walls" of glass brick under cabinets and strips of narrow windows over top cabinets, or using glass-paned or French doors in lieu of solid ones.

Skylights, set either directly overhead in light wells or flush in cathedral-style ceilings, are excellent at lighting up a dreary kitchen. Today's plastic skylight surfaces dramatically increase the intensity of the natural light yet render it soft and diffuse. Skylights—like windows— have become energy-efficient, minimizing heat gain, energy loss, and glare. (See

ABOVE: **A contemporary masterpiece, this kitchen uses broad expanses of glass to pull in the panoramic view.** LEFT: **An arching, highly decorative window not only reveals the view, but frames it in brilliantly dramatic style.**

more about windows and skylights on pages 128–131.)

If you wish to increase natural light in your kitchen, you first need to know the room's sun exposure. Observe where the sun hits the room, and at what angles, during various times of the day—and remember that the angle of the sun changes with the seasons. Southern exposures generally offer the best light. West-facing windows will generate a lot of afternoon light—and heat—something a Sunbelt kitchen will want to avoid. East-facing windows provide good early-morning light, while northern exposures offer little or no direct sunlight.

It may not take much to improve your kitchen's light. Simply adding a second window can boost natural light and make it more even and pleasant. Light-toned cabinets, counters, and flooring will reflect and intensify available light. Or you can bounce light off a light-toned ceiling with louvers or operable blinds (ideally, locate the window fairly high up the wall).

High-reflectance paints bounce more light around than regular wall paint—just be aware that they may increase glare. One trick is to install a "light shelf" (a flat board positioned like a shelf) across the window, located about 12 inches down from the window's top; when painted with a high-reflectance paint, this can throw a great deal of light off the ceiling.

Of course, with more and larger windows, you gain more of an outdoor view. Rather than just sticking a window over the kitchen sink, decide which part of the kitchen should be graced by the view. Through selective window placement and thoughtful use of window coverings, you can screen out unwanted views while emphasizing vistas you wish to enjoy.

TOP: **Generously sized windows are often the best way to bring in natural light, particularly when they stylishly contribute to the kitchen's ambience.** ABOVE: **When windows have a poor view or offer inadequate light, skylights can come to the rescue.**

brilliant solutions Kitchens large and small take on new luster when walls dematerialize and the visual boundary between outside and inside is blurred. As these kitchens demonstrate, storage space need not be sacrificed to expanses of windows in the process. LEFT: Glass-front cabinets become light panels when perched against a clear glass background. The natural light shines through to illuminate colorful glassware, which mingles with glimpses of the garden outside. BELOW: Storage and display turn art form, and the effect couldn't be more stunning. The serene glow surrounding the cooktop and hood in this kitchen is actually a wall of glass cabinets with frosted doors.

creating

a sense of space

IF YOU'RE LUCKY ENOUGH TO HAVE A large kitchen, your main task will be to break up and define the space so it feels comfortable. Even a small kitchen can feel spacious by employing the right tricks—some as easy and inexpensive as using the right paint. Make sure you take into consideration the following basics before you finalize your design.

Even a decent-sized kitchen can seem small and cramped if it's dark. Light defines space, so adding windows is the perfect way to light up the kitchen during the day and visually enlarge the space by opening it to the outdoors. If your kitchen has only one exterior wall, a greenhouse window over the sink is a relatively inexpensive way to add both depth and light. Even if you don't add more windows, consider replacing the existing ones with taller versions that extend the view upward. Installing skylights is a similar way to open up the kitchen "box." You can maintain the sense of spaciousness at night by illuminating the kitchen with undercounter lighting and with task lighting, which creates a sense of volume.

A more involved—and expensive—method of creating a sense of space is to eliminate nonessential structural elements that impede sight lines into other spaces or otherwise give the kitchen a sense of being enclosed. An island or peninsula in place of a wall or half-wall maintains a kitchen's boundaries while establishing visual continuity to an adjacent room or rooms. Non-load-bearing walls can be eliminated easily and fairly inexpensively, but even load-bearing walls can be pierced to create openings or pass-throughs that allow the eye to see past the wall into another space. Raising the ceiling, or even opening the kitchen to the floor above, can make a small kitchen seem downright voluminous.

Light colors make a room look larger, so consider them for paint, flooring,

countertops, and cabinets. Also, using semigloss paint will reflect light—and it's easier to clean. Glass-fronted cabinets add depth, as does undercabinet lighting.

Creating a sense of space in your kitchen, however, can also mean bringing it a sense of definition by providing focal points or highlighting certain areas or elements to command attention. For example, if you like to have guests around while you cook, you can establish a cook-

ABOVE: **Exposed beams can frame a large open area.** OPPOSITE: **Think of space in terms of volume, not perimeter. Breaking through to the roofline with a window will help to expand the sense of space.**

ing "stage" by framing a cooktop island with columns. A built-in breakfast nook will help delineate the separation of eating area from food-prep area. Stenciling can mark the boundaries of an open-plan kitchen, and subtle changes in paint tint can distinguish areas without contracting the space visually. A strategically placed peninsula can demarcate a kitchen boundary without enclosing the space, while second sinks and dual prep areas can create distinct work spheres.

ABOVE: With no walls and no drop ceiling limiting the view out or up, this traditional kitchen forms part of a spacious "great room" that combines kitchen, dining, and living areas. Skylights and recessed lights that flank the ceiling spine illuminate the total volume. LEFT: "Supersizing" windows and rough-hewn tree-trunk beams brings a potentially overwhelming space down to comfortable proportions.

ABOVE: An open expanse is brought under control when the space is broken up by an island and a dining table set parallel to each other and to one counter. LEFT: Creating a sense of space can also mean creating drama through structure. In this case, the cooktop "stage" is established by the presence of substantial wood pillars.

family kitchens

LET'S FACE IT—IF YOU HAVE KIDS, YOUR lives revolve around the kitchen. But a true "family kitchen" is more than just a kitchen with a family parading through it. Today, designers and homeowners are creating multipurpose kitchens that become the hub of the entire house.

These homey kitchens combine traditional food-prep, cooking, and cleanup elements with casual dining areas and eating counters, homework and home office spots, even laundry facilities, allowing the homemaker to consolidate daily tasks into one efficiently planned space, all while watching the kids.

The "family kitchen" is by no means a new concept. For centuries, families have built lives around combined kitchen/dining/living areas—the colonial "keeping room" or "great room" is a perfect example. Certainly, today's family kitchen benefits from a generous amount of openness and space, but this kind of kitchen is more about literally bringing the family together

A family kitchen offers a friendly and casual space for breakfasting, snacking, or studying for school.

to share home life. The key to a successful
family kitchen is its ability to entice everyone into a common space where tasks can
be accomplished individually *and* experi-
ences can be shared. For that reason, family kitchens often orient task areas to face a
central point, so family members can inter-
act as they work.

At its simplest, a family kitchen allows
cooking and eating in the same space.
The once-revered kitchen table is making
a comeback, often joined by an island eating counter. Such counters, set at a different height than the work surface of the
island, are great spots for breakfast, lunch,
and snacks. Because they usually overlook

a food-preparation area or cooktop, they
make wonderful conversation centers.
They're also great spaces for reading the
newspaper or doing crafts.

More-ambitious family kitchens provide work areas as well. A computer station can be built into a low counter at one
end of an island or in a nearby wall unit.
Such a workstation built into the kitchen
is a wonderful asset—whether providing
an electronic file box for recipes or serving as a secondary desk for kids, who can
get homework help while you cook.

Another labor-saver is to locate the
laundry area either immediately adjacent
to the kitchen or behind paneled doors

**The ability to multitask
is a family kitchen's
mandate. This elegant
kitchen effectively
combines areas for
cooking, dining, and
office work, and con-
tains a cook's library
as well.**

within the confines of the kitchen itself.

A well-designed family kitchen also encourages family members to share in the food prep and cooking. Young children can benefit from undercounter fold-down or pullout step stools and graduated counter heights that help cut the kitchen down to their size. You might even want to incorporate a children's art area—for example, a small, low-set counter, perhaps an easel, with built-in storage for supplies, and, of course, display space for the kids' masterpieces.

A family kitchen, needless to say, is a well-trafficked place that will undergo a good deal of wear and tear. Choose easy-clean, resilient materials such as composition counters, vinyl or hardwood flooring, and heavy-duty washable fabrics or slipcovers for chair cushions and upholstery.

A television is a staple in today's busy family kitchen. Here, the TV pops out from behind hideaway doors on a pullout shelf.

the "great room" A cozy dining table that blossoms from the end of a peninsula serves as the transition point between the kitchen proper and the adjacent family room. A modified "great room" setup such as this, which is perfect for a family with young children, allows the cook to supervise the goings-on while preparing and serving a meal. Smart organization puts the cleanup sink and dishwasher adjacent to this dining area, while a second, smaller food-prep sink sits in the island. A clever space-saver in this design: using the dishwasher as the table base.

Warm, casual, homey—
this spacious family
kitchen/dining/sitting
room has spatial and
emotional links to the
colonial "keeping room."

heart of the home This open and airy kitchen concentrates its primary work surface on a massive central island, which offers easy access and viewing to the sitting room beyond. The absence of walls between these traditionally segregated areas encourages family members to mingle even as they do their own tasks. Such amenities as the cheery window seat in the kitchen and the cantilevered counter at the island's end ensure company for the cook. Increasingly popular, such open plans acknowledge what all families already know: The kitchen is the heart of the house.

born to entertain

IF YOU'RE AN ENTHUSIASTIC COOK who loves to entertain, you probably enjoy company while you work. For you and those who share your interest in entertaining, today's kitchen designers have broken down the walls between kitchen, dining, and living rooms to create one large entertainment space, where guests can mingle with the cook while the meal is prepared, and even served, right on the spot.

The entertainment kitchen is a unique hybrid that has the openness and friendly ambience of a family kitchen yet usually is more elegant in style. Often the centerpiece of the kitchen's design is a dramatically sculpted island equipped with the cooktop facing into the room, an elevated bar area with counter stools, and a sweeping buffet/serving surface. The kitchen is likely to be just one area of a comfortable room filled with couches, chairs, small tables suitable as perches for plates and wine glasses, and perhaps a fireplace. Lighting is usually on dimmers to modulate the mood as the evening progresses.

If you want to make your kitchen the focus of your entertainment space, you will have certain style considerations. The kitchen and seating areas should blend seamlessly—for example, the cabinetry in kitchen and adjoining areas should match or be complementary, and you may want to lay a single type of flooring throughout the whole area. The decor of the rooms should also match. In other words, if your seating area is modern and formal, your kitchen should be, too. If you prefer a cozy south-of-France feel, the kitchen area should reflect country-French style as well.

A multipurpose island may be worth its investment in terms of visual impact and efficiency, but a well-positioned peninsula that serves as bar/buffet also can be effective for a smaller area. You

Eliminating wall barriers, literally and visually, between kitchen, dining area, and patio gives guests room to roam.

may want to include an undercounter wine cooler and wine storage racks, or incorporate a formal bar setup with bar sink, cabinets or racks for beverages and glasses, and perhaps a small refrigerator. An uncluttered buffet area, with a fluid traffic path, is essential.

The cooktop or range is the heart of the entertainment kitchen, so you will want to make it as efficient an area as possible. Eye-catching overhead hanging racks and undercooktop open shelving can position pots and pans exactly where you need them. Organize your essential cooking tools, spices, and food-prep items in drawers adjacent to the cooktop, and add pullout shelves next to the cooktop to

handle prepared and cooked foods.

You will also want to minimize the unsightly side of cooking—the pre- and post-cooking messes. To that end, consider including refrigerator drawers in the island for easy access to meats and produce, as well as an extradeep pot sink directly behind the cooktop for quick dirty-pot cleanup.

Kitchens built for entertaining are often the most beautiful, mainly because their owners invest in high-end materials and custom details. Glass, stainless steel and other metals; pricey woods such as mahogany, bird's-eye maple, and teak; and granites and marbles often highlight these luxury spaces.

This peninsula widens to provide an extragenerous buffet or dining counter, allowing a good view of the proceedings while buffering the cook from too much foot traffic.

The cook becomes part
of the party when the
kitchen adjoins an open
sitting area, and the
centralized cooktop,
which faces the bar,
offers seating as well.

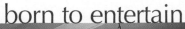

pass-through efficiency When the cook prefers a bit of privacy and a more formal dining arrangement, an old-fashioned pass-through may be just the ticket. This modern take (shown from both sides) offers a panoramic view of the stylish kitchen. A classic molding on top allows it to display art as well.

An eat-in kitchen need not be a casual affair. This elegant combination-island design provides both intimate seating for two and grand buffet service for a crowd.

island kitchens

THE ISLAND HAS ENJOYED GROWING popularity in kitchens over the last decade, and for good reason. It's doubtless one of the kitchen's most versatile elements. Its antecedent, the kitchen table, worked—and continues to work—effectively as a baking and food-prep surface, but the island is capable of so much more.

An island can be shaped or sized to fit practically any kitchen's contours. It can be wrapped around a load-bearing post or angled to face an adjoining room. And it can have more than one counter height—a surface higher than a conventional counter for casual dining or lower for bread-making and pastry work. It can be plumbed with a second sink for food preparation, wired for electrical appliances, and have gas lines and vents installed for cooktops or grills. In fact, installing a cooktop or sink in an island is a great way to shorten the distances between key work areas of the kitchen triangle.

A large multipurpose island may include a cutaway for barstools, undercounter wine refrigerator, drawers, shelves, and enough work surface for a family of cooks.

The island can also serve multiple roles simultaneously. A parent can prepare dinner while a child snacks or does homework at the island counter, or two cooks can work at the same time at opposite workstations. The right island can serve as a bar or an elegant buffet, with food dished up hot from the cooktop. A generous island can host a computer station or telephone desk, an undercounter wine cooler, a warming drawer, a small refrigerator, and more.

Most islands are storage powerhouses, often for lesser-used appliances, pots and pans, and serving pieces. If you cook on the island, however, the cabinets nearest the cooktop should hold the most-used pots, pans, and utensils. Open cabinets in the island can house a cook's library, display attractive pottery or baskets, and store an adjacent family room's television and electronics equipment.

Islands generally are fixed in place, but in smaller kitchens, a movable island on locking wheels, with collapsible side panels that swing up for dining, may be a better choice. Installing in-floor electrical outlets increases the versatility of a movable island even more.

The best kitchen layouts for an island are one-wall, L-shape, and U-shape floor plans (see pages 58–61). When installing a permanent island, size it in proper proportion to the kitchen. You will need to leave a 48-inch clearance from island to counters for safe passage—more if two cooks will be working simultaneously. Also make sure the lighting is sufficient; install at least one light for every task area on the island. If you use the island frequently for entertaining, a dimmer switch will allow you to set mood lighting.

Since the island usually serves as a kitchen's focal point, it should be in step with your kitchen's overall style. It also lends itself to key decorative touches such as an eye-popping cooktop hood or a wrought-iron pot rack that can complete the look of the kitchen.

This island, as decorative as it is serviceable, combines open and closed storage.

shaped to fit Conforming to the plan like a slice of pie, this quarter-round island serves up the pièce de résistance for a small but elegant kitchen. Its straight sides provide plenty of work area along the kitchen's counters while its arc eliminates a projecting corner. This is a good example of how even a small kitchen can benefit from an island that's suitably proportioned.

An imaginative freeform island undulates through the center of this kitchen, showing how it can be the room's most versatile component. Cooktop and hood are centralized at one end of the countertop "pool," which puddles into generous open space for food prep, dining, or simply a place to keep the cook company.

A parallel pair of sizable islands are more than a study in symmetry. They create two separate work areas with a generous space in between for the two-cook family.

A "boomerang" island is a stylish and convenient setup for a bar or buffet. It sets the tone for the adjacent curvy counter-tops that soften the kitchen's edges.

This hardworking island's counter curves to mimic the ceiling's unusual form. In addition to hosting the hungry, the island features a cooktop, wine rack, and plenty of storage.

island powerhouse This freeform multilevel island is many things to many cooks, in fashionable style. In addition to food-prep counter space, it houses a cleanup sink and dishwasher, a smooth-top range, and a well-lit bar/dining area. As if that weren't enough, it has plenty of cabinets and drawers, making it a true storage workhorse.

layouts that work

IF YOU'RE TAKING ON A MAJOR KITCHEN remodel, you may have the opportunity to reconfigure your kitchen's layout to make better use of its space. Regardless of a kitchen's size, only a handful of layout shapes are successful at utilizing space. These shapes are classified with names that are self-descriptive: one-wall, galley, L-shape, U-shape, and G-shape. Each configuration has its strengths and weaknesses, usually measured by the efficiency of the so-called kitchen triangle—a design concept that sets the optimum distances between sink, cooktop or range, and refrigerator (see page 60).

Today, the classic triangle is modified—or turned into a polygon—by factors that didn't exist when the concept originated, including multiple-cook kitchens that require additional workstations, and a multiplicity of work focal points, such as toaster oven, microwave, and dishwasher. Nevertheless, the kitchen triangle principle is helpful when evaluating basic floor plan options.

Your home's overall floor plan may dictate which layouts are possible, but if you have some flexibility, study how your family operates in and around the kitchen to hone the best plan.

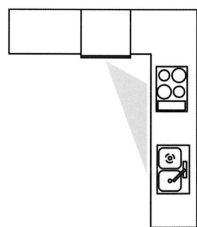

In the L-shape kitchen, placing the refrigerator, range or cooktop, and sink in close proximity maintains efficiency and also keeps the walking to a minimum.

The space-saving galley kitchen can be dark and claustrophobic, but those problems vanish with natural light sources along one wall and at the corridor's end.

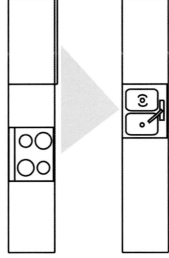

With a one-wall kitchen, the classic triangle becomes more of a rectangle. An efficient answer to a small-space kitchen area, this layout is usually the product of necessity. Adding an island makes the kitchen more workable and allows the cook better interaction with guests.

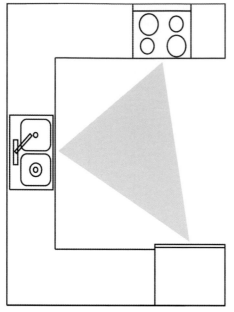

the kitchen triangle

The three most important work areas in the kitchen are the refrigerator, cooktop or range, and sink. Arrange these in an efficient work triangle with individual legs no longer than 9 feet and no shorter than 4 feet. The sink should be at the center of your work path, between the refrigerator and the range; allow at least 2 feet of counter space on one side of the sink and at least 18 inches on the other. Situate the refrigerator at the end of a cabinet run near an access door, and allow at least 15 inches of nearby counter space as a staging area for groceries. For food preparation, allow 3 feet of counter space alongside the cooktop or range; for two cooks, double that amount. If your plan includes an island, make sure to place it at least 42 inches away from work centers.

LAYOUT	ADVANTAGES	DISADVANTAGES	NOTES
ONE-WALL Sink, cabinets, and appliances located against one long wall.	Keeps kitchen area to a minimum and leaves it open to the room. Good for entertaining.	More walking, since "triangle" components are in a row; prepping, cooking, and cleaning are done with the cook's back to the room.	Addition of a small island across from the sink and between the stove and refrigerator facilitates cooking and allows the cook better interaction with guests.
GALLEY Two parallel walls, with entry and exit at each end.	Compact; efficient triangle easily achieved by placing one major appliance on opposing wall; easy access to cabinets.	Difficult for more than one cook; space can feel cramped if the corridor is not wide enough; family traffic through the space can be disruptive.	Locate refrigerator and microwave near one end in order to minimize traffic flow through the work space.
L-SHAPE Two adjacent walls.	Accommodates two cooks; makes setting up an efficient triangle easy, with minimum traffic interruption; easily accommodates island.	If cabinet runs are too long, can require a lot of walking; all work done with the cook's back to the room.	An island works well in this layout if the area is spacious enough; since the corner is prominent, consider storage options to avoid dead space.
U-SHAPE Three adjacent walls.	Considered by many the most efficient layout since stove and refrigerator usually face each other, with sink at the base of the "U"; generally can accommodate two cooks.	Corners can be dead space, dark and claustrophobic, depending on the light sources and cabinetry finish.	Use lazy-Susan corner cabinets to maximize storage; consider large windows and/or skylights; keep the color scheme light.
G-SHAPE U-shape with a peninsula at one end.	Favored by the serious cook or by two-cook households, since it offers space for multiple workstations (for example, food prep, special baking area, indoor grill); discourages traffic.	Can feel too closed-in, especially in smaller kitchens with dark cabinetry; restricts view to other rooms.	Keep colors light and work areas organized; if small, do not add an island.

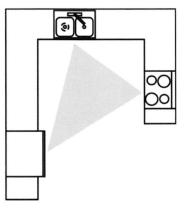

Open shelving, glass-fronted cabinets, and a bank of windows keep this small U-shape kitchen from feeling cramped.

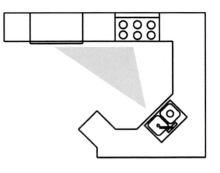

The short, jutting peninsula turns this U-shape kitchen into a G, creating a handy spot for serving or dining.

universal and accessible

THE REVOLUTION IN KITCHEN DESIGN over the past several years has brought with it a new flexibility that allows for accommodating those with special needs. That includes not only persons with physical impairments but an increasingly aging population as well. The result is the development of "universal" and "accessible" design principles that are worth getting to know, particularly if you intend to grow old in your home, if you plan to have an elderly parent come live with you, or, of course, if someone in your family is physically challenged.

Although the terms "universal" and "accessible" tend to be used interchangeably, they refer to slightly different things. Universal design focuses on enabling people of different ages and physical skill levels to function well in the kitchen. The goal of accessible design is a "barrier-free" layout—according to guidelines set by the federal government—that allows the wheelchair-bound access to all of a kitchen's facilities. Both principles contain good ideas that, in some cases, may be adapted to kitchen designs for those with no special needs.

The best kitchen layouts for easy movement are L-shape or U-shape, with at least a 32-inch entry-door width—sufficient clearance for a wheelchair. A wheelchair-bound person also requires a minimum of 5 feet turning clearance between counters, or counter and island, or counter and table. Other essential accommodations include lowering the sink counter to about 32 inches and using a sink no deeper than 6 inches, creating a 27-inch clearance for legs and knees; in addition, undersink pipes should be enclosed or insulated to prevent legs from getting scalded.

Upper cabinets also should be set lower, with bottoms 15 inches above countertops. Side-by-side refrigerators and the

Varying counter heights enable the elderly and infirm to sit, or stand without bending, to accomplish tasks.

A bottom freezer is a boon to the elderly, since it saves bending for refrigerated goods.

design

new refrigerator drawers provide easy access to goods; undercounter microwaves and lowered ovens aid cooking. Pullout shelves adjacent to stove, refrigerator, microwave, and dishwasher help with heavy items. All electrical outlets and light switches should be located between 15 and 48 inches from the floor.

If you are designing with an elderly person in mind, or simply in anticipation of your later years, one of the simplest things you can do is include counters of varying heights. Islands are particularly good for this since they can have more than one level. The variety allows you to sit while doing some tasks and to do others without having to bend. An elderly person may also benefit from a refrigerator with the lesser-used freezer on the bottom, pullout shelving to make retrieving pots and pans easier, and blade-style faucets that eliminate the need for turning handles. Look for appliances with large digital displays, and timers that emit loud beeps or buzzes. Keep distances from sink to refrigerator to stove at a comfortable minimum. Last but not least, make sure there is good lighting throughout with switches that are easy to find and reach.

If these principles interest you, you can obtain universal and accessible design guidelines from the National Kitchen & Bath Association (NKBA) at www.nkba.org, as well as from the federal government's American National Standards Institute at www.ansi.org.

Blade-style faucets, which can be elbow-operated, spare arthritics and other manually impaired persons painful movement.

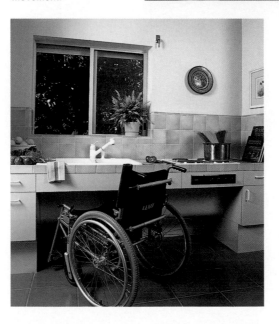

This smart setup gives the wheelchair-bound necessary undercounter leg space to access both sink and cooktop.

organizing and

TODAY'S KITCHEN—WHICH HAS BECOME
a dynamic workspace where one or more
cooks must be able to operate quickly and
efficiently—demands highly organized
cabinetry and work centers. If the kitchen
is small, it's critical to take advantage of
every inch of space and to minimize clutter. If the kitchen is large, proper organization can help cut down the need for
traipsing from one work area to another.

If you haven't kept up with develop-
ments in kitchen cabinetry, prepare to be
delighted as you peruse the new "smart"
cabinets and their many storage options. A
cabinet's interior is critical to organizing
your kitchen resources. A variety of cabi-

**The rhythmic mix of
closed and open
shelving is echoed in
the sculptural island in
this open kitchen space.**

storage

net organizers are discussed here; you'll find more information on pages 88–89.

kitchen zones

The easiest way to organize your kitchen is to break it into different task areas, according to the functions you'll perform there. Think in terms of four key centers: sink, cooking, refrigerator, and preparation.

In addition to the sink, the sink center includes a dishwasher, garbage disposal, trash compactor, and the cabinetry necessary to store dishes, glassware, cleaning supplies, a chopping board, and other food-prep utensils.

At the heart of the cooking center is the range or cooktop; ovens may be nearby but out of the way. Store pots and pans, racks, cooking utensils, and pot holders within easy reach of this area. Locate your microwave near the refrigerator, since most items that go into the microwave come from the refrigerator. Place the cooktop or stove close to the sink to ease the filling and draining of pots and pans.

The refrigerator center calls for counter space and pantry areas. Unloading and putting away groceries is easier the more centralized you make food storage. Also store foil, plastic wrap, and freezer containers in a nearby drawer or cabinet.

A preparation center may not seem necessary but can be very handy; in fact, you may want more than one for different tasks. This is a good place to store small appliances, cookbooks, recipe boxes, canisters, mixing bowls, and the like. Ideally, your baking oven or ovens should be situated near this area. If you have a food-

prep sink, perhaps set in an island, locate it near the refrigerator for quick transfer of items. Keep the equipment needed for food preparation—food processor, blender, colander, salad spinner, mixing bowls, knives, oils, and spices—in nearby cabinets and drawers.

The time you spend thinking through how your kitchen should be organized will pay off in spades at your project's completion. If you do your planning right, your kitchen can't help but stay organized, because the organization is built right into it.

Good storage need not be all about built-ins. Inexpensive store-bought islands can add both work and storage space to existing cabinets.

smart cabinets Today's "smart" cabinets are a brave new world of specialized organization possibilities. TOP ROW: With recycling an everyday part of life, cabinets and even drawers are able to divide and conquer kitchen refuse cleanly and efficiently. MIDDLE ROW: Organization is partly artful concealment. A bar or tea service can disappear behind an appliance garage door, a pantry behind a sliding door, and a roll-out cutting board and storage cart under a counter. BOTTOM ROW: Articulated shelving can break clutter down into easily accessible goods. Pullout shelves and drawers can separate the potatoes from the onions and the flour from the sugar, and give utensils and spices their own sense of space.

Solid walls of cabinets, although useful, can be bland, or, at worst, claustrophobia producing. This kitchen avoids that trap by punctuating the space with beautifully illuminated display cabinets, including one that cleverly minimizes the island's mass.

Islands and peninsulas, especially when they are long and wide, can be storage powerhouses. Mixing closed and open shelving reduces any sense of bulkiness.

This small kitchen takes advantage of every nook and cranny, including perching the television on top of the microwave shelf. The angled food-prep station also houses knives and extends out far enough to become an eating counter.

expert efficiency

WHEN YOU'RE REMODELING A KITCHEN, it pays to remember that this is first and foremost a workspace where you should be able to prepare meals and clean up afterward with ease. Fortunately, there are time-tested guidelines for designing an efficient kitchen, and plenty of conveniences created with cooks as well as looks in mind.

An effective kitchen layout is a huge energy-saver because it puts everything you need within easy reach. Once you've mapped out your basic floor plan, you'll be able to add amenities that fit your lifestyle. If you entertain often, a second dishwasher or a pass-through for transporting food to the dining area might be welcome. An island or bar could be a boon if meals at your home tend to be grab-and-go. And wouldn't the family sous-chef appreciate an extra sink or an auxiliary food-prep area?

Retooling your kitchen will also give you the chance to create cook-friendly storage space. Install deep drawers under the cooktop for easy access to pots and pans, shallow ones near the dishwasher so clean flatware won't have far to go. Put a built-in knife rack near the cutting board, or a backsplash rack near the range so you won't have to hunt for your spices. You can even take advantage of awkward spaces: A corner base cabinet can hold a recycling center or a lazy Susan, and a deep countertop makes a perfect site for an appliance garage.

Contemporary materials make it easier than ever to design a kitchen that's both functional and beautiful. Easy-care surfaces for floors and countertops can save you countless hours of upkeep. Resilient flooring, now more stylish than ever, wipes clean in a jiffy and is affordable

Angling both the sink and the adjacent countertop makes quick moves around a small space a breeze.

expert efficiency

and gentle on the feet as well. Elegant solid-surface countertops resist stains and can be sanded to remove small blemishes and scratches.

Today's appliances offer every sort of convenience a cook could want. Duel-fuel ranges have the flexibility of a gas cook-top and the reliability of an electric oven. Smooth-top electric ranges make cleanup a cinch. Refrigerators can be equipped with temperature-controlled storage units that keep food fresher, as well as pass-through shelves that allow access to items inside without opening the door. Dish-washers with sensors can tell how dirty the dinner plates are.

Keep in mind as you plan your kitchen that what works for others may not work for you. If you tend to set sizzling pots all over the place, you won't appreciate a solid-surface countertop, which can crack when overheated; if you have young children, you may not want a smooth-top range that remains hot after you've turned off the burners; if you haven't baked a pie or roasted a turkey since the Reagan administration, you won't be needing a pastry counter or a convection oven. Remember—the point is, remodeling is all about providing the workspace that works for you. When it comes to kitchen efficiency, you're the expert.

This stylish multilevel peninsula is many things to many users: food-prep, food-service, and dining counter.

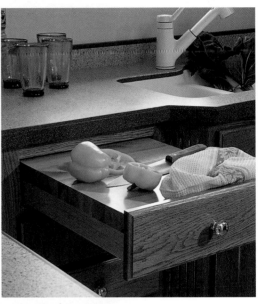

LEFT: Behind an elegant curved door, stacked metal-topped swing-out shelves house a baker's resources. BELOW: A pullout butcher block adjacent to the sink is perfectly situated for smaller cutting tasks.

Tapering grooves cut into a sloped dish drainer in a solid-surface countertop quickly and cleanly carry away liquids to this extradeep cleanup sink.

decorative details

WHILE YOUR CABINETS LARGELY SET the style of your kitchen, it's the little things—the personal touches and design details—that give your kitchen its personality. Cabinet pulls and knobs, paint treatments, fixtures, clever use of countertop and flooring materials: These small-scale, but critical, choices turn an ordinary kitchen into something special.

Just about any facet of the kitchen can be enlivened by the right touch. A country kitchen's plain-lined cabinetry becomes even more evocative if given a distressed paint finish and chicken-wire door panels. Old-style linoleum or an artful mix of square vinyl flooring tiles adds just the right accent to a '50s design. And today, it is easier than ever to find just about any style of plumbing or lighting fixture to suit your kitchen's look.

Maximizing a style's design potential through use of the right details is just one way to spice up your kitchen, however. Sometimes it takes only one small but significant element to pack a design punch. For example, in recent years, cabinet hardware shapes, sizes, and materials have exploded into an exciting selection of tiny items that can make remarkable visual impact. Some, usually crafted of stainless steel or chrome, are as sculptural and decorative as jewelry pieces. Others, often of brass or pewter, are whimsically shaped like animals, vegetables, or even forks, knives, and spoons. There are solid industrial-style knobs and pulls for high-tech kitchens, and beautifully rendered copies of vintage patterns for traditional kitchens. The choices are endless, and you will find the search for the perfect accompaniment to your cabinetry as entertaining as it is worthwhile.

Paint treatments are another fine source of interesting kitchen detailing. Stenciling is an easy, inexpensive way to add a focal point to a kitchen's look. You can, of course, be more elaborate. Trompe l'oeil

Alternating solid and patterned tilework is a detail that sets the whole kitchen's tone (see opposite).

("fool the eye") painting can create a "virtual" window with a view or a stylish still life over a counter. Paint is one of the least-expensive design materials, so it's worth experimenting with different colors and color combinations until you find the perfect look.

Decorative ceramic tile is another relatively inexpensive material that can bring personality to a cooktop wall or stretch of counter backsplash. The possibilities, again, are seemingly endless. Ready-to-assemble tile murals and other prefigured tile combinations are an eye-catching way to bring life to your kitchen design.

As you choose these final touches, try to find one item or element that will be unexpected—a conversation piece. How about a chandelier made of cups and saucers with dangling spoons, an elaborately arched faucet set between plain-lined cabinets, or a coat of brilliant red paint on an otherwise light-toned cooktop wall? These are the decorative details that will enhance your enjoyment of your kitchen, and the more idiosyncratic they are, the more your personality will be on display for others to enjoy.

The confluence of perfectly coordinated details—earthy variegated tile, subtly toned cabinets, distinctive cabinet cutouts, and diminutive pendant lighting—harmonizes and personalizes this kitchen's unique design.

decorative details

LEFT AND BELOW: Small pieces of rough-and-ready stone, set in decorative patterns and repeats, are elegant details that lighten the expanses of rustic stone backsplash and flooring.

ABOVE: A country kitchen gets a true taste of the farm when chicken wire fronts plain-lined cabinets, an inexpensive yet highly evocative detail. RIGHT: Even a pet will enjoy whimsical detailing—as long as the food is good.

designing with tile Ceramic tile remains one of the best sources of interesting design details, especially when budget is a consideration. Elaborate tile murals such as the one above make a bold presentation that demands appropriately low-key cabinets and countertops as a foil. Such complex murals can be pricey, but a handful of highly decorative expensive tiles, set in an expanse of inexpensive "field" tiles, also can make a design splash.

buyer's guide

WHETHER YOU'RE UPDATING YOUR KITCHEN WITH A SIMPLE FACELIFT OR GIVING it a complete makeover, you will be faced with countless decisions. Thousands of products are waiting to be dropped into your shopping basket or carted off the showroom floor. Even if you're an avid shopper, selecting appliances, fixtures, flooring, and other materials can be daunting—particularly when you consider that many of these are big-ticket items that you'll be living with long term.

It isn't enough just to know what you like: There are technical questions and construction issues to consider, as well as such practical concerns as whether your new refrigerator will fit into the space you have in mind—and fit into your budget.

Indeed, every decision you make may seem to raise a new set of questions. You know you want maple cabinets, but should you buy European style or traditional? Should your superquiet dishwasher have a stainless-steel interior? Should your new six-burner cooktop be gas or electric? The challenge is to find kitchen elements that suit your taste, your space, your lifestyle, and your pocketbook. And they should be products that will serve efficiently and reliably for years.

This chapter is fashioned to help you make these choices. It gives you information about the vast array of products out there, so you can decide for yourself which ones are right for you.

Once you know what you're looking for, a Lowe's consultant can show you a wide selection of products that are perfect for your project. Lowe's even has designers on hand to assist you with your choices, and at the same time you make your purchases, you can arrange for installation.

kitchen cabinets

Cabinet configurations and storage options come in an almost unlimited array of designs and finishes.

SINCE CABINETS DOMINATE A KITCHEN design and usually account for nearly half the cost of a major remodel, it pays to do your homework before making a purchase. When you set out to shop for cabinets, you'll find a staggering array of types, styles, and prices. You can streamline the process if you begin by determining what look you like, including the style, and what price point is comfortable for you.

Regarding price, you can choose relatively affordable mass-produced stock cabinets, pricey made-to-order custom ones, or midrange "semi-custom" hybrids. Or you can mix mostly stock cabinets with a few custom ones to create your dream kitchen on a budget.

Be sure to order cabinets early in your

remodel, since appliances, countertops, and sinks cannot be installed until cabinetry is in place.

cabinet construction

There are two basic methods of cabinet construction: "faceframe," in which the front edge of the cabinet box is concealed by a 1-by-2-inch hardwood frame, and "frameless," sometimes also known as "European style."

About 80 percent of the cabinets made by American manufacturers are of the faceframe type. Because the structural frame makes it possible to use lower-quality wood for the cabinet sides, faceframe cabinets can be less costly than comparable frameless ones. However, the frame also narrows the openings of drawers and doors, which means you'll have less storage space. Faceframe cabinets are a good option if your kitchen walls aren't quite straight (which is the case with most older kitchens), since the frame can be shaved to fit an irregular space.

European-style cabinets are constructed of panels that are finished on both sides, so cabinet boxes butt right against one another. Because there's no space-gobbling frame, almost the entire cabinet box can be used for storage. A separate toe-space pedestal (plinth) allows you to vary counter heights or stack base cabinets to make tall cabinets. Most frameless cabi-

nets use the "32-mm system," which means that holes are drilled at intervals of 32 millimeters along each side panel so that hardware such as door hinges and shelf pins can be plugged in anywhere you like. Since nearly all manufacturers of frameless cabinets use the same system, components are interchangeable.

Easy-to-clean white laminate offers a crisp look in European-style frameless cabinets.

FACEFRAME CABINET

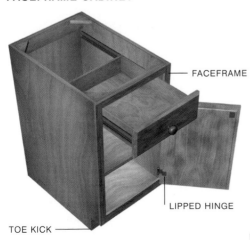

FACEFRAME

LIPPED HINGE

TOE KICK

FRAMELESS CABINET

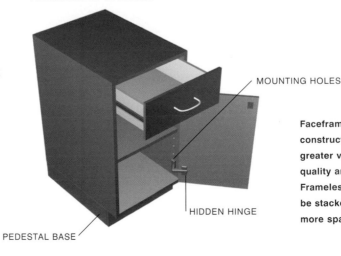

MOUNTING HOLES

HIDDEN HINGE

PEDESTAL BASE

Faceframe cabinet construction allows for greater variation in wood quality and pricing. Frameless cabinets can be stacked, and have more spacious interiors.

Solid-maple raised-panel doors with a natural finish and concealed hinges distinguish these stock cabinets.

stock cabinets

If your budget or your schedule is tight, stock cabinets offer many advantages. Because they are mass-produced, stock cabinets cost at least a third less than cabinets that are custom-made or configured to order, and they are usually delivered in less than three weeks.

However, stock cabinets do have limitations. Since they're manufactured in standard sizes, they may not be the ideal

choice for an unusual space or an innovative kitchen plan. Your selection of styles and finishes is relatively restricted, and special accessories such as breadboards, wine racks, and roll-out shelves might not be readily available or available at all.

That said, stock cabinets can be used in just about any kitchen. There are so many standard sizes that it's usually possible to accommodate even an unusual installation: Widths vary in 3-inch (continued on page 82)

MAPLE

- A hard, close-grained wood
- The texture is fine and even
- Predominantly off-white in color with yellow-brown hues
- Can feature "bird's-eye" dots; grain is mostly straight but may be wavy

CHERRY

- Close-grained with a uniform texture
- A warm hardwood that mellows as it ages
- Color can vary from pale yellow to deep reddish brown within one panel
- Natural or light stains accent color variations; streaks and small knots are common

OAK

- Grain patterns run from straight to widely arched
- Color ranges from white to yellow to reddish brown; variation can be strong within a panel
- Mineral deposits add color accents of cream or black; wormholes or knots may be present

HICKORY

- Strong, open-grained wood
- Dramatic, flowing grain patterns
- Wide variation in color from blond to deep brown
- Distinctive burls, streaks, knots, and wormholes

LAMINATE

- Very smooth surface in white or cream colors
- Durable finish and easy to maintain
- Color may change over time; panels can either be flat or raised

LEFT: A breakfast nook is enhanced by the dramatic addition of ceiling-to-floor glass display cabinets.
ABOVE: Dark-stained hickory cabinets are set off by a ceramic-tiled backsplash and deep red walls.

kitchen cabinets

increments, from 9 to 48 inches; upper cabinets are available in heights of 12, 18, 24, 36, and 42 inches for use over sinks, stoves, and countertops. Manufacturers also offer a wide variety of designs, features, and finishes. For an additional cost, some will even make modifications to their cabinets, allowing you (within a certain range) to increase or decrease cabinet depths, alter toe kicks, or upgrade interiors or doors.

A trip to your local Lowe's will give you an idea of the many choices available in stock cabinetry. You'll find dozens of styles, from country cottage to contemporary, plus hundreds of options for personalizing your installation with hardware and decorative touches (for more tips on how to give your cabinets a "custom" look, see "Creating a Custom Look," opposite).

custom cabinets

Custom cabinets are designed and built from scratch to fit a particular kitchen. Consequently, they cost a great deal more—five to fifteen times more, depend-

This room's warmth comes from natural and stained oak cabinets, mullioned glass doors, and plank flooring.

Birch storage, display, and service areas form a unique arrangement in this charming indigo-stained kitchen.

ing on the materials and sizes—than stock cabinets. You may also spend six weeks to three months waiting for them to arrive. It's worth the wait and the money, however, if your goal is to transform your kitchen into a showpiece. Skilled cabinetmakers can create heirloom-quality woodwork that can't be made by machine.

semi-custom cabinets

If you want special sizes, configurations, or finishes, semi-custom cabinets may serve your needs without breaking the bank. Semi-custom cabinets are manufactured, but you have as many as 2,000 stan-

CREATING A CUSTOM LOOK

With a little creativity, you can achieve a made-to-order look using afford-able stock cabinets. Here are a few tips for creating a custom-made appearance without spending a fortune:

- Add options, such as glass doors, display shelves, or plate racks.
- Order specialty accessories through a cabinetmaker.
- Ask the manufacturer to sell you prefinished plywood and hardwood pieces that match your cabinets. It's also possible to have pieces fabricated to create special cabinet parts such as fillers, soffits, and angled connections.
- Outfit your refrigerator and dishwasher with decorative panels that match the cabinets.
- Vary cabinet heights to avoid a "prefab" look.
- Replace stock door and drawer pulls with more-interesting varieties.

kitchen cabinets

base cabinetry features Base cabinets offer such specialty options as sliding trays (shown), as well as storage compartments for dry staples or a built-in lazy Susan. The interiors should feature easy-to-clean laminate surfaces. Adjustable board shelves also come in handy. Standard base cabinets range in width from 9 to 48 inches; they are 24 inches deep and 34½ inches high. The box construction on the base cabinet shown above features ⅜-inch-thick plywood, which wraps around the entire case. The plywood shelves are ¾ inch thick. The surface of the cabinet is durable and nonpeeling. Solid wood doors and drawer fronts are available in maple, cherry, and other hardwoods.

dard options from which to choose. If you still can't find what you want, you can ask for just about any modification imaginable, including oddball sizes, specialty accessories, and custom colors or finishes.

You'll pay more for semi-custom cabinets than you would for stock cabinets, but you'll often get higher-quality workmanship and materials: For example, the semi-custom cabinets designed especially for Lowe's customers feature solid-wood dovetail construction, supertough finishes, and extrathick shelves that exceed industry standards.

Delivery of semi-custom cabinets can take a couple of months, so place your order well in advance. The Lowe's kitchen specialist who helps you select and design your cabinets can also give you a reliable delivery date.

ready-to-assemble cabinets

A less-costly cousin of stock cabinets, RTA (ready-to-assemble) cabinets are sold knocked-down in flat boxes for assembly by the customer. Despite their rock-bottom prices, RTAs can be quite stylish and versatile. Most are frameless "European-style" cabinets, and are relatively easy to put together and modify. You'll only need basic tools and respectable do-it-yourself skills to tackle the job. However, if you're uncertain of your abilities, hire a Lowe's specialist to do the installation.

RIGHT: **Adjustable, low-profile hinges give a clean, uncluttered appearance to kitchen cabinetry.** FAR RIGHT: **Solid ½-inch wood drawers feature dovetail joinery—a sign of fine construction.**

LEFT: **The elegant decor of this room is achieved by cherry paneling and fluted island pillars.**

LEFT AND ABOVE: **Sleek white finishes and bright interiors distinguish kitchens of white laminate cabinetry. Styles range from contemporary to country and are scratch-resistant.**

kitchen cabinets

cabinet refacing The fastest, thriftiest way to update your cabinets is to reface them rather than replace them. With refacing, the cabinet boxes stay in place and are simply repainted. Then new doors and drawers are added. The process is economical not only because you don't incur the expense of new cabinets, but also because countertops, wall coverings, plumbing, and wiring are left untouched. Refacing is relatively simple for experienced do-it-yourselfers; if you don't have the talent or time, you can arrange for Lowe's to do the work. Consider refacing only if your cabinet boxes are in good shape and you're satisfied with your kitchen layout. A wide selection of materials is available for stylish resurfacing jobs. Crafted hardwoods or laminate cabinet doors and drawer fronts undergo quality control procedures and are custom fitted to the measurements of your particular kitchen.

ABOVE: **This kitchen appears new by benefit of cabinets refaced with solid wood doors and drawer fronts.** LEFT: **Door options include Shaker, Southwest, Cathedral, and Roman Arched with raised or flat panels. Affordable laminate doors are a practical choice. A variety of woods and stains are offered, while brackets, valances, and other decorative accents can be integrated, too.**

storage accessories

IN THE QUEST FOR KITCHEN EFFICIENCY, cabinet manufacturers have learned to think inside the box. Most offer a range of accessories that lets you customize your cabinet interiors to suit your needs.

There are cabinet accessories for just about every purpose. Some increase your kitchen's storage capacity, others make kitchen items more accessible; some even give you additional workspace.

Accessories that turn wasted space into storage are among the most useful you can add. If you have a corner base unit, you can outfit it with a lazy-Susan or a recycling carousel; the unusable countertop recess above can accommodate an appliance garage. A straight corner base cupboard can hold a garbage bin or a set of semicircular wire trays; when attached to the back of the cupboard door, the trays will pop out automatically once the door is opened.

Racks and pullouts will boost storage space and make it easier to see what's inside your cabinets. Rolling shelves on heavy-duty drawer glides will give you easy access to pots and pans at the back of a base cabinet, and you can add a shallow pullout above for pot lids. Narrow shelves affixed to the backsplash or the inside of a cabinet door will put spices and condiments close at hand. A pantry unit with full-length folding racks or pull-out shelves will provide two-sided storage and keep inventory in sight.

Look for specialized cabinet accessories that will simplify the tasks you perform every day. Preparing and serving meals will be easier if you have a built-in knife rack near the cooktop, a cutting board that folds down from the backsplash, or a plate rack that makes everyday dishes more accessible. Cleanup goes more quickly when you have a pullout storage tray that keeps cleaning supplies in order under the sink. You may want a drop-down cookbook holder or a tilt-down drawer for sponges to control countertop clutter, or a slide-out trash bin to keep garbage behind closed doors. Built-in canisters for flour and sugar and vented bins for potatoes and onions will streamline the search for ingredients.

You'll have no problem ordering accessories for almost any style of cabinetry. And, if you have purchased your cabinets at Lowe's, it will be easy to add extra organizers in the future.

The fun of remodeling is picking your storage options. Here, choices include spice racks, base "Susans," and a slide-out garbage bin.

LEFT AND BELOW: **Vertical and horizontal storage rolls out of these base cabinets, providing instant organization and access to pots, pans, and beverages.**

The pure function of a hidden wire bin (ABOVE) contrasts with an open cabinet with rustic pull-out baskets (RIGHT).

cabinet hardware

ALTHOUGH HARDWARE IS OFTEN AN afterthought, it can make a big difference in the way your kitchen looks and functions. The right knobs and pulls can spruce up old cabinets or add polish to new cabinetry. Choosing decorative hardware is mostly a matter of taste: Look for something that appeals to you and suits the style of your kitchen. You can find knobs and pulls shaped like teacups, seashells, dragonflies, or just about anything else that strikes your fancy, and at Lowe's you can get hardware crafted from mango wood, carved resin, hand-cut glass, and other specialty materials.

Make sure your selection has a durable finish that won't wear off with repeated use, and remember that pulls will look especially prominent because they occupy more cabinet surface than knobs do. If

ABOVE: **Figurative hardware such as these birdhouse pulls in polished aluminum can define or unify a kitchen theme.**
RIGHT: **Pulls and knobs in scrolled form and black iron finish complement light-wood cabinets.**

you're simply replacing your hardware, it's a good idea to look for knobs or pulls that will fit the existing holes in your cabinet doors (take along samples of your old hardware when you go shopping). If your new hardware doesn't match your old, you'll need to fill the holes or cover them with a backplate.

The hinges inside your cabinets ensure that doors remain stable and easy to operate. Before you shop for hinges, make sure you know whether you have faceframe-type cabinets or European-style frameless ones (see page 79). You'll also need to determine what kind of cabinet door you have. Some hinges are made to fit only one type of cabinet and one style of door. Others are more versatile.

A partial wraparound hinge not only can be used on all faceframe cabinets but has a large surface area that improves door stability. Self-closing European hinges can be used on both faceframe and frameless cabinets, and you can adjust them to align and level cabinet doors. Ease of installation and the ability to handle heavy doors make the European hinge the most popular on the market.

Hinges are specified for use on right- or left-hand doors, and they come in different sizes to support different door weights. In addition to choosing the proper hinges, you'll need to determine how many it will take to stabilize each door. Use the chart at bottom right to make your calculations.

Unless you've chosen self-closing hinges, you'll need to outfit your cabinet doors with catches. Catches use either magnets or tension to hold doors closed. Magnetic catches work well on irregular or warped doors. Spring-roller and friction catches close quietly and keep doors shut securely.

For drawers that function smoothly, choose hardware sturdy enough to support the drawer and its contents. Drawer slides have load ratings of light, medium, and heavy, so make note of each drawer's

likely contents before you shop. You'll also need to measure the length of each drawer to determine how long your slides should be. Drawer slides come in side-mounted or center-mounted styles; while center-mounted slides are more affordable, side-mounted styles are considerably more durable. If you choose side-mounted slides, you can add options such as drawer stops, ball-bearing or nylon rollers, self-closing designs, and slide extensions that allow access to the entire drawer.

Cabinet hardware is not just a pull or knob but can be a great expression of one's own personal style—muted, whimsical, minimalist, or flamboyant.

HINGE REQUIREMENTS

DOOR HEIGHT	DOOR WEIGHT	HINGES
40 inches or less	11 pounds or less	2
40–60 inches	12–20 pounds	3
60–80 inches	21–33 pounds	4
80–85 inches	34–48 pounds	5

countertops

WITH THE EXCEPTION OF FLOORS, NO household surface undergoes more wear and tear than—or is as noticeable as—a kitchen countertop. Fortunately, many durable and beautiful options, in a wide array of materials, colors, and finishes, are available today.

A standard countertop is 25 inches deep and 1½ inches thick; it is set 36 inches above the floor. When installed on a standard base cabinet, it will overhang in front by 1 inch.

Because most kitchen walls are slightly out-of-square, the safest course is to order your countertops after you've ordered your base cabinets. Have your Lowe's professional create a template when you order your countertop.

The chart on page 95 lists the most popular types of countertops, from the least to the most expensive.

backsplashes

A backsplash is the short wall area that runs along the back of a countertop. It may be a separate piece or integral with the countertop.

Despite its relatively small size, a backsplash is likely to be one of the first things to catch your eye when you enter a kitchen. Because a backsplash offers big visual impact but requires only a bit of finish material, it is an ideal place to express your creativity.

A backsplash has only one practical requirement: It must be easy to clean and durable enough to scrub over and over again because it receives the bulk of splattered food from cooking.

If a backsplash is not integral to the countertop, it should be installed last because it will almost certainly require detailed work around electrical outlets, switches, and other obstacles.

If the backsplash will have horizontal lines, such as grout lines on a tile installation, check regularly during installation to make sure they align with the wall cabinets and countertop.

Backsplash choices include all of those for countertops: plastic laminate, ceramic tile, wood, solid surface, and stone.

Plastic-laminate and solid-surface

Square and diamond patterns in this tile counter and backsplash combine elegantly with this kitchen's Shaker-style base cabinets.

LEFT: **Some solid-surface countertops consist largely of quartz, which renders them stronger than stone. Surfaces are completely waterproof and color choices span the rainbow.**

RIGHT: **A confetti-speckled countertop in a lemon-colored room is one design choice among hundreds. Laminate and solid-surface choices mimic wood, granite, and even glass.**

RIGHT: **A ribbon of "rock" adds visual interest to this sleek, seamless counter.** BELOW: **High-gloss mini-tiles provide fun design options; they are durable and available in many colors.**

Plastic laminate comes in an enormous palette of color and style choices, from solid shades of white, smoke, blue, and burgundy to fired, burnished glazes; patterned wood grains; marble; and colored slate.

materials will likely be integral to the countertop, and with no seams they will be a joy to keep clean.

Ceramic and stone tiles are installed just the same as the countertop, but they do not need to be as thick or strong because they will not receive the same wear and tear. However, make sure they are well glazed or sealed for stain resistance and easy cleanup.

Wood is suitable only for a backsplash molding and will need to be resealed periodically. Be sure to purchase pieces that are prefinished for use in a kitchen, or apply several coats of clear polyurethane finish after installation.

Your easiest and least-expensive option is either paint or wallpaper. A high-quality semigloss latex paint offers enough water and stain resistance for most kitchens. Choose scrubbable wallpaper. Paint or paper the wall before installing the countertop and any backsplash molding.

TYPE & ADVANTAGES	DRAWBACKS	INSTALLATION
PLASTIC LAMINATE Available in a large number of colors, patterns, and textures. Very durable and easy to clean. "Color core" laminate is worth the extra expense because it resists minor scratches. "Post form" has curved edges, with an integrated backsplash and slightly curved drip-resistant front edge.	Once damaged—plastic laminate can burn or crack—it is all but impossible to repair. Seams, especially at inside corners, can be hard to keep clean. Flush or undermounted sinks cannot be installed in it.	Post-form countertops require gluing the plastic laminate onto particleboard, a challenge for even an experienced do-it-yourselfer. The backsplash can be sanded or cut to make up for out-of-square walls.
CERAMIC TILE You can let your imagination run wild with the wonderful assortment available. High-quality tile is virtually burn-proof and very difficult to scratch. If a tile cracks, it can be replaced.	Grout between tiles can be difficult to keep clean. Irregular surfaces can cause glasses or china to chip or break more easily if dropped.	Tile must be installed on a solid, water-resistant underlayment—typically, ¾-inch plywood topped with ½-inch cement backerboard (see pages 214—217 for step-by-step instructions). Order 10 percent more tile than needed for breakage.
WOOD Wood is naturally beautiful, resilient, and easily reparable. Dropped glasses and china have a better than even chance of survival, and chips and scratches in the surface can be sanded and refinished. Maple is the most popular choice, but any hardwood will work.	Because wood is easily scratched and burned, resist the temptation to use it as a cutting board or landing pad for hot pots and pans. Wood must be sealed with bar wax or a similar product every few months to prevent water damage.	Buy the lengths you need and simply cut to fit. If you wish to install an undermounted sink, you will need to cut the hole for it precisely and waterproof the edges to protect them from moisture. A self-rimming sink is an easier option.
SOLID SURFACE Extremely durable, almost impossible to chip or burn. Scratches can be sanded away. The easiest material to keep clean. Many colors and patterns available. Sink can be formed right into the countertop to create an "integral sink."	High prices and, for some brands, limited choices. Can be cracked by hot pots and pans. If the countertop is badly damaged, replacement is expensive because of it being one integral piece.	Most types can only be installed by a certified professional who is contracted by the manufacturer.
STONE Granite, limestone, slate, and marble are commonly available; granite is the most popular. Hard stone is difficult to scratch, resists most stains, and does not require a surface sealer. Granite tiles can be installed in much the same way as ceramic tile and cost far less than installing a solid granite slab.	Granite slabs are very expensive. Marble easily stains but when polished is a perfect choice for a baking center. Even very hard, polished stone tends to be slightly pitted and porous. Limestone and slate may absorb stains.	Stone slabs should be installed by a professional; however, you should inspect a variety of slabs to choose the one that appeals to you. Make sure the installers polish all exposed edges.

Resilient floors come in numerous styles and colors and can complement almost any decor. A urethane surface coating offers protection against dulling as well as scuffing.

kitchen flooring

A KITCHEN FLOOR SHOULD HAVE THE durability and beauty to emerge from constant traffic, food spills, and dropped dinner- and cookware looking brand-new. Fortunately, quite a few products on the market today meet this challenge.

If cooking is one of your passions, and you also love the look of ceramic or stone tile, be aware that those surfaces will be harder on your legs, a plate or glass dropped on them will likely shatter, and a dropped pot may damage the floor. On the plus side, these surfaces are easy to clean, requiring little more than a swabbing with a wet mop.

Wood and resilient flooring are kinder to the legs, and dropped items have a chance of survival. If you choose wood, make sure it is hardwood and ask about how to take care of it. Resilient flooring is almost foolproof, but again, ask for specific guidelines on how to maintain it.

installation considerations

Most new flooring can be installed on top of a floor that is slightly springy, such as an existing laminate floor. However, before installing ceramic or stone tile, have a large adult jump on the floor; if you detect any flexing, the floor will need reinforcing. The underlayment should be at least 1¼ inches thick, total (for example, ¾-inch plywood topped with ½-inch backerboard). Joists should be no farther than 16 inches apart. If you are unsure of your underlayment, call in a carpenter.

If your floor is more than ¾ inch out of level in any direction, or if there are noticeable dips, it may need structural improvements—or at least an application of self-leveling compound—before you install new flooring.

If your proposed kitchen floor will be more than ½ inch higher than an abutting floor, it could pose a tripping hazard. In that case, select a threshold that comple-

This glazed-porcelain-tile floor, in almond, has a lightly distressed surface resembling quarried stone.

flooring

VINYL SHEET OR TILE

Vinyl (and polyurethane) flooring is highly popular because it is both tough and resilient underfoot and available in a wide range of colors and patterns. Some styles convincingly imitate other materials, such as wood or stone. Available in 6- and 12-foot-wide rolls and in 12-inch-square tiles. Where durability is critical, opt for solid vinyl rather than surface-printed varieties.

Vinyl can be torn, burned, dented, and scratched. When damaged, individual vinyl tiles are easily replaced (be sure to purchase extras), but sheet flooring may require complete replacement. Tiny imperfections in the underlayment may show through the surface over time.

The underlayment must be perfectly smooth and free of dirt. In most cases, it's best to have sheet vinyl professionally installed. Installation of vinyl tile is relatively easy for do-it-yourselfers, as discussed on page 200.

OTHER RESILIENT FLOORING

Beyond vinyl, resilient flooring materials suitable for kitchens include linoleum, cork, and rubber. All are soft and quiet underfoot and relatively easy to install and maintain. Most are available as 12-inch-square tiles. Linoleum, long wearing and available in many fashionable hues and patterns, is an environmentally sound choice because it's made from natural materials. Cork is also an environmentally sustainable product. Rubber is highly stain resistant, soft, and extremely quiet.

Linoleum, cork, and rubber can be torn, burned, dented, and scratched. Plus, compared to vinyl, they can be pricey. Tiny imperfections in the underlayment may show through over time. In a kitchen, cork must be sealed and won't hold up as well as other resilient products. Though rubber is available in several colors and textures, selection is limited.

Methods are similar to those used for vinyl (see page 200). The underlayment must be perfectly smooth and free of dirt. You'll want to have linoleum and sheet products installed by a professional.

CERAMIC TILE

Tile comes in every color under the sun. Porcelain has a glasslike surface that is impervious to water and stains and is easy to wipe clean. It will be slippery when wet unless it is textured. Quarry tile is unglazed but is usually hard enough to resist water. Terra-cotta and Mexican saltillo tiles have a soft, earthy look.

Check carefully to ensure the tile will stand up to spills and scratches. Unglazed quarry tiles should be sealed at least once; softer tiles on a regular basis. Make sure the grout is properly sealed.

The underlayment must be very strong; it's best to install cement backerboard as an underlayment (see page 202). Apply latex-reinforced thinset mortar using a notched trowel, and set the tiles using plastic spacers to ensure consistent grout lines. Fill the joints with latex-reinforced sanded grout, and apply grout sealer after grout cures.

STONE TILE

Natural stone—including marble, granite, slate, travertine, and limestone—offers a casual yet elegant look. Stone may have a glossy surface, or it may be "honed" or "sandblasted" for a softer look. Properly cared for, stone tiles can last generations.

All stone except granite is porous and will permanently stain unless a sealer is applied. Because some stones are easily scratched, you'll want to test them before buying. Stone can be cold underfoot and hard on the legs.

Prepare the floor and install as you would ceramic tile. Stone must be cut with a wet saw. Some stone (especially marble) is slightly translucent, so use white thinset rather than gray mortar.

HARDWOOD STRIP FLOORING

Available in random lengths, from 1½ to 3 inches wide, most hardwood flooring is milled with tongue-and-groove edges that fit together tightly. Maple, oak, birch, and bamboo are available, as well as wood-look laminate floors.

Installation of natural hardwood is time-consuming. Also, the wood must be well protected. If the flooring is unfinished natural wood, it must be sanded, stained, and finished.

For conventional hardwood, the underlayment need not be very strong or very smooth. Install as discussed on page 206. For more about laminate "floating" floors, see page 209.

ments the flooring on both sides.

There are two basic types of thresholds to consider. With a flush threshold, which is at the same height as the new flooring, the flooring must be cut to meet it precisely. An on-top threshold spans the joint between the two surfaces, so your cuts do not have to be precise.

A metal-strip threshold is the easiest to install; it easily accommodates a difference in flooring heights. Be aware that it may not be the best aesthetic option if the transition is from wood to tile. However, if your new flooring will abut carpeting, it is the perfect solution.

A hardwood threshold is beveled on both sides for easy cleaning. Install it with screws, and then seal it well with a polyurethane finish.

Marble and other thresholds made from stone are available premade, or they can be special-ordered.

An "antiqued" laminate plank floor is weathered with saw marks, nail holes, knots, and textured crevices.

paint and wallpaper

THE QUICKEST WAY TO MAKE A DECOR-ating statement is to paint or paper your kitchen walls. However, don't take either task lightly. A poorly covered wall may peel or appear dingy in a year or so. To do the job right, you must carefully choose materials and use techniques appropriate for your walls.

Bright yellow paint combined with "white-wash" highlights the sunny aspects of a traditional kitchen. Semigloss paints that are stain- and mildew-resistant are best.

choosing paint

Paint for walls and woodwork is either latex (water-based) or oil/alkyd (solvent-based). For many applications, latex paint is now the standard choice because new formulations perform as well as oil/alkyd paints and are more environmentally safe.

However, oil/alkyd paint is still considered the best choice for painting cabinets because of its adhesive properties and smoothness of application.

Ranging from dull to shiny, paint lusters are flat, eggshell, pearl, satin, semigloss, and gloss. The lower the luster, the better it will hide surface imperfections and the more difficult it will be to clean; glossier paints show defects but are scrubbable. Semigloss and satin are the most common choices for kitchen woodwork; lower-luster pearl and eggshell are popular for walls and ceiling. Choose the luster that best suits the location.

The extra cost of high-quality paint is money well spent. When buying latex, choose paint that is 100 percent acrylic. It retains its original color long after other paints have dulled, it sticks securely, and it has a surface that stays glossy, for easy cleanup. A paint that guarantees one-coat hiding (read the fine print) can save you plenty of time.

Paint the ceiling with the same paint you use on the wall. Avoid "ceiling paint," which is very flat, because it will soak up cooking stains like a sponge.

For those who want something a little extra special, the kitchen is a great place to apply a faux finish. Applying two or three colors using techniques such as sponging, ragging, and dragging will give a feeling of depth to a wall so that the kitchen will feel larger even if the paint is dark. Or consider creating a handcrafted look by stenciling walls or cabinets. You can purchase stencils from a craft store or create them yourself.

LEFT: **Newly painted trim, walls, and cabinets make a striking difference. Dollar for dollar, painting is the most effective improvement you can make.**

ABOVE: **In this country kitchen, walls are painted "stone," the chest "deep yellow." A wallpaper border of lemons ties the color scheme together.**

Before making any wholesale paint purchase, buy a small quantity and apply it on two or more walls. Examine the paint at various times of the day and night. A room's light source, cabinetry hues and texture, and other factors can seriously affect a paint's effective color.

choosing wallpaper

The moisture and odors inherent in a kitchen make it a natural enemy of wallpaper. For this reason, you do not want to compromise on quality.

Vinyl wallpaper is the most waterproof; however, design and color options are limited. Metallic or foil wall coverings are moisture-resistant, but because they are tricky to install, you may want to rely on the services of a Lowe's professional. Embossed paper with a glossy finish will repel modest amounts of moisture and stand up to occasional wiping, so if your kitchen is not heavily used, this may be a perfect option for you.

At all costs, avoid inexpensive wallpaper. It will stain and peel off easily. Wallpaper made of natural fibers will soak up stains and should also be avoided in the kitchen. Be sure that all wallpaper rolls are from the same dye lot since different lots may have significant differences in hue. To give yourself the option of re-papering or painting later, choose "strippable" wallpaper and buy a few extra rolls.

As for pattern, though wallpaper is commonly associated with a country look, there are designs that can complement a sleek, modern decor. Unless your kitchen is very large, buy light colors and small prints, which will visually enlarge the space. Vertical stripes and patterns will make a room appear taller.

kitchen sinks

THE KITCHEN SINK IS ONE OF THE most heavily used fixtures in the home. Even if you rely on a dishwasher, you probably work at the sink at least an hour each day. So buy a sink that is durable, pleasing in appearance, and easy to clean.

When you shop for a sink, you'll quickly learn that sink designers have been busy in recent years. A trip to Lowe's will reveal not only a complete variety of materials, but a vast selection of depths, sizes, configurations, and even colors.

The standard sink is 22 by 30 inches, with two equal-sized bowls 8 inches deep. If you frequently use large pots, you will appreciate a 9- or 10-inch-deep bowl. For peeling and washing vegetables, you'll find that a small shallow bowl at the sink's

This triple-basin task, or cuisine, sink comes with accessories to turn it into a complete prep workstation as well as a cleanup area.

A clay-fired under-mount sink designed to resemble mosaic tile has a very durable high-gloss finish.

center can be a handy choice.

Most sinks have four holes for mounting faucets and accessories. Other hole mounts include a faucet's sprayer, a hot-water dispenser, a spout for a dedicated water filter, the air gap for a dishwasher drain, and a liquid-soap dispenser. If the sink you want doesn't have enough holes for the devices you desire, look into special ordering one. (You can drill a hole in a stainless-steel sink using a special metal-cutting hole saw.) If you don't need all the holes in the sink you wish to buy, ask about matching plugs for capping the unused holes.

In addition to choosing a material and bowl configuration you like, make sure you consider how the sink will be installed and seated. A self-rimming sink rests on top of the countertop; this is the easiest installation, but crumbs can collect where the sink meets the countertop. An

Flowing lines common to china and cast-iron sinks grace this rolled-rim stainless-steel model.

kitchen sinks

undermount sink attaches to the underside of the counter; though the installation is more difficult, this setup is significantly easier to keep clean.

Here's a closer look at the kitchen sink materials you're most likely to find:

STAINLESS STEEL Available in a wide range of prices, but you get what you pay for. A cheap sink is made of thin metal—you can feel it flex if you push on a bowl, or a garbage disposal may vibrate noisily; plus

A composite sink of quartz and acrylic resin is rock hard, easy to clean, as well as stain- and chip-proof.

This stainless-steel 8-inch-deep bowl with satin finish is constructed with ledges for water containment.

A double-corner sink in stainless works well on an island or countertop corner.

Paired with a high-tech faucet, a composite sink with a "granite" finish has a very contemporary look.

it's easily scratched, has a finish that is hard to keep clean, and may make a drumming sound when you run water into it.

A higher-quality sink is thick and firm, and its finish will maintain its original appearance if you simply wipe it clean.

Avoid a sink with a "mirror finish." It looks great at first, but water spots will be a constant headache, and scratches will soon mar its appearance.

Check the insulation on the underside of the bowls, which is intended to deaden the sound of running water. Foam insulation works better than sprayed-on.

ENAMELED CAST IRON Has a smooth, elegant finish unmatched by any other sink material. Available in many colors. The finish is very hard and rarely chips. Running water will hardly be heard, and hot water will cool slowly. Easiest of all materials to clean; just a wipe will usually restore the original luster.

Avoid enameled-steel sinks, which resemble enameled cast iron but do not perform well.

COMPOSITE Acrylic and fiberglass are not recommended because they soon lose their glossy finish and absorb stains readily. Newer composite sinks have a more durable finish. "Quartz" sinks, composite sinks with a high quartz content, are especially durable.

However, even the best composite sink is susceptible to scratching. Avoid using abrasive cleaners or allowing sand or dirt to get rubbed onto the surface. Running water will make a drumming sound, though not as loud as in a stainless-steel sink. Push down on a bowl to make sure the sink is firm; if it flexes, a garbage disposal may vibrate.

INTEGRAL SOLID SURFACE A solid-surface countertop can be ordered with a molded sink, either in the same color or a complementary hue. The sink can be scratched, but the damage is easily fixed.

You'll find the greatest choice of color in cast-iron sinks. An enamel finish is thick, glossy, and tough, yet lends itself to graceful design.

ABOVE: **This undermount sink is constructed of 12-gauge stainless steel.**
RIGHT: **A round bar sink with a "quartz" composite bowl can also be used as a secondary kitchen basin.**

SPECIALTY SINKS

In addition to the standard sinks discussed here, consider a secondary sink to ease the task of food preparation and cleanup.

DECORATIVE An extra-pretty sink can be pricey and may be difficult to keep clean; however, it just may add that special touch that transforms a plain kitchen into a conversation piece.

VITREOUS CHINA Made of molded clay fired at a very high temperature, these sinks commonly have ornamental designs and come in unusual shapes. Most do not have mounting holes, so the faucet must be installed in the countertop. The finish is easy to clean and nearly impossible to scratch or stain. It can, however, chip, so beware of bumping it with pots or pans.

BRASS AND COPPER Sinks made of these materials are usually for bathroom use, but may be appropriate as a secondary sink. They should be wiped dry after each use to prevent tarnishing.

ANTIQUE An antique sink can lend a kitchen the pleasant ambience of a farmhouse. Many older sinks are composed of one large deep bowl with an attached drainer—an arrangement some people prefer—and tend to be quite sturdy.

BAR Positioned near the cooktop or next to a cutting board, a bar sink can be used for cleaning vegetables or other food preparation. Before enlisting it to fill large pots with water, be sure it's deep enough.

kitchen faucets

A KITCHEN FAUCET GETS TURNED ON and off and has its spout swung side to side thousands of times a year. How long a faucet will put up with this abuse with little or no maintenance depends largely on the quality of its inner workings.

In a cartridge faucet, the main component is a cylindrical cartridge with passages and rubber O-rings that allow water to pass through when the handle is turned. Models with brass cartridges usually just need the O-rings replaced every few years. A plastic cartridge will wear out in time.

The body of a ball faucet has inlets with little spring-loaded metal seats. The

RIGHT: **An elegant single-handle faucet is complemented by a matching liquid-soap dispenser and spray nozzle.** BELOW: **Classic style merges with modern hardware in a levered spout with brushed nickel finish.**

ball presses down on the washers to shut off the water. When the handle is turned, a ball rotates to allow water to pass through one or both inlets. A metal ball will be extremely long lasting, while a plastic ball may need to be replaced a lot sooner. Eventually, the springs and rubber parts will wear out.

When you turn the handle of a ceramic disc faucet, two discs made of hard ceramic rub against each other to seal or open water passages. The disc itself is usually long lasting and will wear out only if you have mineral-laden water. Rubber seals will eventually wear out.

faucet features

Many faucets are the two-handle centerset type, with a base plate that spans across three sink holes. A two-handle widespread

model—often used to achieve an ornate look—has a spout and two handles that are mounted separately. The most practical choice for a kitchen is a single-lever faucet, which allows for quick, easy temperature adjustment with just one hand.

A standard centerset faucet with a separate sprayer requires four sink-mounting holes. Other models require three, two, or even just one. Make sure your sink has enough holes for your faucet.

Choose a spout design that suits your sink and your cleanup needs. Its length should allow you to swivel it while water is pouring out without the motion causing undue splashing.

A faucet with a pullout spout/sprayer, sometimes called a "one touch," is convenient and reliable. Beware of the two-handle faucet with a separate sprayer, which is notoriously unreliable.

You can also buy a filtering faucet, which looks like a regular faucet but includes an undersink water filter. You simply push a button or lever to deliver filtered water out of the spout. The filter's cartridge must be changed from time to time; some models have an electronic indicator that tells you when. You can also buy filtering faucets that allow easy sink-top replacement of the filter core.

finishes

Most faucets have spouts, bodies, and cover plates made of brass plated with a finish material—often a shiny polished chrome. Bright chrome is easy to wipe clean but shows water spots readily. Brushed or satin chrome, which has a distinctly mellower appearance, is a bit easier to keep spot-free.

A brass finish presents a stunning appearance but can be difficult to maintain. A high-gloss brass finish may have a factory-applied clear finish that saves you from regular polishing.

Powder-coated enamel comes in white, black, or decorator colors. You'll find it very durable.

TOP: **This French country–style faucet is graced by an antique copper finish and tall arched spigot.** ABOVE: **An easily installed chrome faucet, swivel spout, and spray are the standard in most American kitchens.** LEFT: **A pull-out faucet in disguise, this striking high-arc ceramic disc fixture is available in several finishes, black and white among them.**

dishwashers

DISHWASHERS ARE OFTEN AT THE TOP of the wish list for those remodeling an old kitchen. When the first models appeared, they produced spotted glasses, and dishes needed to be prewashed. New models are quiet, energy efficient, able to dispose of residue, and powerful enough to clean pots and pans.

The standard dishwasher is 24 inches wide, 24 inches deep, and 34 inches high. Compact models, usually 18 inches wide, are also available. Dishwashers can run from a couple of thousand dollars down to a couple of hundred dollars, with the difference in price reflected in the number of features a given model offers.

Here's what to look for:

QUIET Nearly silent machines are now available because of improved sound insulation, sound-absorbing washtubs, vibration absorbers, and low-noise pumps. Top-of-the-line models have all these plus a stainless-steel tub, which is quieter than the usual plastic.

ENERGY EFFICIENCY As a result of federal regulations, today's dishwashers use about half the electricity of earlier machines. Much of this improvement is due to water conservation. Newer dishwashers use less water (typically about half that used when washing by hand) and, therefore, need to heat less water.

A stainless-steel interior is pricier but more efficient during the drying cycle. And, because metal reflects heat better, less energy is used. Of course, the air-dry option is the most energy efficient.

EXTRA-HOT WATER Older models simply used water directly from the hot-water

BELOW: **A touch pad and microprocessor control temperature, cleaning and rinse cycles, and delay options.** BOTTOM RIGHT: **This dishwasher contains an insulation package to help minimize noise.**

supply pipe, which meant that dishes washed in lukewarm water if the hot-water supply was depleted. Many of today's models have an option that heats the wash and rinse water to 140 degrees before the cycle begins. Manufacturers recommend 120 to 140 degrees for a normal load; some models have a sanitize option that heats water to 155 degrees. This temperature sterilizes dishes, baby bottles, canning jars, and the like, and steam-cleans the grease off crusted grills, range grates, and pots and pans.

REMOVING FOOD RESIDUE Most newer dishwashers eliminate the need to rinse dishes before loading. Filters have improved, and many models now have a small built-in garbage disposal (sometimes called a "hard-food disposer") that grinds and then flushes away food residues. However, it's best to rinse dishes with a lot of tomato residue before loading because tomato products can stain the dishwasher's plastic interior.

CONTROLS These are more user-friendly than ever. Electronic controls, which add to the price, are the norm, but manual controls are still available.

"Delay start" lets you program the dishwasher to start at a later time—for instance, during the night instead of at peak energy hours.

Cycle choices let you tailor the cycle to the contents of your load. The gentle cycle is safe for washing china and crystal (unless it's hand-painted or antique). The heaviest cycle will handle just about anything.

RACKS Some models have adjustable racks. Also look for fold-down trays and adjustable or removable tines.

FINISH Exterior finishes include enameled steel (white, black, or almond), stainless steel, and black glass. Most models offer a replaceable panel in a wider range of colors to blend with base cabinets.

Panel-ready models in wood or laminate let you customize your dishwasher to match your cabinets.

LEFT: **Large-capacity tubs accommodate an assortment of cookware. Flexible racks and foldaway tines can be positioned to cradle tall pots or protect china and stemware.**

undersink fixtures

BECAUSE A KITCHEN SINK IS HOOKED up to the house's water supply and drains, its location is a natural for small kitchen fixtures that use or treat water. Here we look at three such fixtures: garbage disposals, water filters, and hot-water dispensers. With all three of these, what you see at the top of the sink or counter is only the tip of the iceberg; it's under the sink where the main equipment is located and the real action occurs.

garbage disposal

If your disposal will receive steady use, it's worth the investment for a unit that delivers at least ½ horsepower. A disposal with ⅓ horsepower can get stuck digesting fibrous foods and fruit pits and will likely need replacing after a few years.

Check for insulation that keeps the noise down; generally speaking, the fatter the disposal, the quieter it will run. However, make sure it will fit comfortably under your sink.

A disposal is either hard-wired or plugged into a 120-volt box or receptacle. Most people choose to install a switch near the sink, but you can also buy a "batch-feed" model that kicks on when you engage its lid.

Most garbage disposals fit standard drain outlets and are a cook's best friend. Don't clog them with fibrous foods, such as celery or potato skins, or with fruit pits.

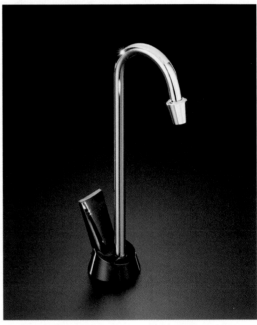

This undersink water filtration system includes an easily installed twist-on/off filter cartridge. The unit delivers fresh-tasting water at 1.5 gallons per minute.

water filter

If you suspect that your drinking water is unhealthy, contact your local water department for test results. If hard water is a problem, consider a water softener. However, water that is simply bad-tasting can be made more palatable with an easy-to-install water filter.

You'll want to consult with a plumber or your local water supplier for the best type of filter for your water. A small, inexpensive carbon filter will remove chlorine taste and reduce sulfur (which causes water to smell like rotten eggs). A bulkier and costlier reverse-osmosis filter will eliminate nearly all bacteria as well as harmful chemicals.

Flexible lines that join with compression fittings lead from a cold-water shut-off valve (or saddle tee valve) to the filter, and from the filter up to a sink-mounted spout. Install the filter's tank within easy reach for changing cartridges.

hot-water dispenser

A hot-water dispenser typically produces 190-degree water almost instantly. That's hot enough to cook thin asparagus, prepare a gelatin dessert, or make tea.

A small heating tank under the sink delivers water via copper tubing to a spout mounted on the sink or countertop. A tank typically holds ⅓ to ½ gallon of water. The higher the unit's wattage, the more quickly it can recover and heat water after the tank has been used up. Energy use is surprisingly low—about ½ kilowatt hour per day.

Hard water requires a unit with a plug for easy draining once or twice a year. Several spout styles are available for harmonizing with your faucet.

Hot-water dispensers can deliver 60 steaming cups of water per hour for drinks, soups, and hot cereals. The gooseneck spout is handy for filling tall pots.

refrigerators

Trim-kit models accept custom panels from your cabinet manufacturer. Factory-installed selections are also available.

EVEN THE MOST ECONOMICALLY PRICED refrigerators available today have significant advantages over older models. They're quieter, do not require defrosting, are easier to clean, and are infinitely more energy efficient.

As a general rule, two people should have at least 10 cubic feet of refrigerator space, not including freezer space. Add 1½ more cubic feet for each additional family member.

Most refrigerators are 28 to 34 inches deep, so they protrude a few inches from cabinets and countertops, which are 24 inches deep. The advantage to this is that the doors do not bump the countertop or cabinets when they open.

If you prefer the refrigerator to be flush with the adjoining cabinets, you may be able to recess it back into the wall, keeping in mind that refrigerators require ventilation. Another alternative is to purchase a shallow "flush fit" refrigerator. With either choice, make sure that the doors will be able to open fully.

Manufacturers have toned it down since the days of avocado and gold refrigerators in the '70s. Economical models are often available in white only; black and almond are sometimes offered. A stainless-steel exterior is pricey but adds an appealing retro look. Some models offer door panels in a wider range of colors and finishes.

The most common type of refrigerator is the two-door top-mount unit—with the freezer mounted atop the refrigerator. The main complaints with this type are that things get lost in the back of the freezer and that the bottom shelves of the refrigerator are awkward to access.

In a bottom-mount unit, however, the freezer—basically a large drawer that slides out for easy access—lies below the

FEATURES TO LOOK FOR

- Large door shelves that can be adjusted. One type of shelf, for example, is just the right size for two half-gallons of milk or juice.
- Glass rather than wire shelves with spill-catching lips.
- Leveling legs to make the unit perfectly plumb and stable.
- Shelves that pull out, fold up and down, or roll up and down (called elevator shelves).
- Racks that dispense pop cans or hold wine bottles.
- In the freezer section, glide-out baskets and shelves, as well as storage space specially sized for large items.
- A freezer light.
- See-through compartment doors.
- Ice/water dispenser. Some are tall enough to accommodate pitchers, and many have water filters. Ice can be ordered crushed or cubed. This feature has long been available in side-by-sides; now it's available in some top-mount models.
- Refreshment center. This little door provides easy access to frequently used items.
- Customized temperature control for different areas—for example, the deli drawer, crispers, butter compartment.

refrigerator. More frequently used refrigerator items are at eye level.

A side-by-side model offers convenient access to both the refrigerator and freezer and makes good use of door space. However, narrow freezers do not easily accommodate big items such as pizzas or turkeys. Also, side-by-sides waste a good deal of energy because their tall, narrow freezer compartments are harder to cool.

Most refrigerators have deep doors. With these, more food items can be accommodated in easy-to-reach door compartments and the main refrigerator is shallower, allowing for easier access.

getting a **built-in look**

A growing demand for models that effectively conceal the presence of the refrigerator in the kitchen has inspired several alternatives, including:

VENEERED FLUSH REFRIGERATOR You can recess a freestanding refrigerator back into the wall so that it is flush with the cabi-

LEFT: **Top-mount refrigerators have freezers at eye level. This model has a roll-out freezer floor for easy access plus an interior ice-water dispenser.** RIGHT: **Bottom mounts work for those who favor the fridge and don't want to bend for fruits and vegetables. Wire roll-out baskets ease freezer access.**

refrigerators

Storage variety is pictured in these side-by-side and top-mount refrigerators: sealed-glass crispers, tilt-out door shelves and baskets, and expandable wire shelves.

nets, then cover it with matching veneer or cabinet panels.

DRAWER COOLER A more expensive solution is a compact refrigerator drawer unit that fits into a cabinet. These models can be paneled to match surrounding cabinets or finished in a sleek contrasting material such as stainless steel or glass.

UNDERCOUNTER MODELS Both refrigerators and freezers are available in compact

This sleek wine cooler stores up to 24 bottles and comes with an electronic thermostat and interior lighting.

sizes to fit under counters. They measure 33 to 34 inches in height, and vary quite a bit in width—18 to 57 inches. Depths are 25 to 30 inches, but trim models are available that will slide into the standard 24-inch-deep base-cabinet runs.

wine coolers

These units maintain the optimum temperature and humidity to keep wine from going bad and to help it age properly. They are available in both freestanding and built-in models and can accommodate from 20 to 60 bottles.

Typically there are two separate cooling zones, for red and white wines. Doors are often made of amber or smoked glass to protect the wine from exposure to light. Some models can be covered with cabinetry panels. Features include slide-out racks, adjustable shelves, digital controls, and security locks.

freezers

Usually, a freezer is placed in the basement or garage and is used for storing bulk items. For those with enough space in the kitchen, an upright freezer can be matched with a single-door refrigerator to create a spacious side-by-side ensemble. This combination offers good energy efficiency because each cooling system operates independently.

Chest or upright? Opening the door of an upright freezer allows plenty of cold air to escape and warm air to enter. If you expect to open a freezer more than twice a day on average, a chest freezer will save you significantly in energy costs. Newer chest freezers have sliding and pullout trays that make it easy to find what you're looking for.

Some models have an alarm that goes off if the temperature dips too low for safe food storage. Many freezers need to be defrosted occasionally; look for one with a drain plug to facilitate this chore.

This efficient chest freezer features 8.8 cubic feet of storage and adjustable temperature control.

Newer refrigerators no longer use CFC (chlorofluorocarbon) refrigerants, which contribute to ozone depletion, making them far less harmful to the environment.

ENERGY TIPS

Next to air-conditioning and heating, a refrigerator is the largest user of electricity in a home. If you have an old refrigerator, a new model likely will pay for itself in a few years. To make your refrigerator even more efficient, follow these simple tips:

■ Develop quick in-and-out habits. Resist the urge to stand and peruse the possibilities with the door open, and enjoin the rest of your family to do the same.

■ Lower the freezer and raise the fridge settings. The lowest you should go for the freezer is 0 degrees; the highest you should go for the fridge is 38 degrees.

■ Check for a tight door seal. A piece of paper should stay snug in the door when closed, even if you tug it. If it slips out easily, replace the gasket.

■ Make sure the condenser doesn't have to deal with dust bunnies. Most condensers are near the floor; remove the coverplate and vacuum all around the bottom of your fridge a few times a year.

■ Keep a full freezer, which makes it easy to keep new items cold. The same is not the case, though, with a full refrigerator, which forces the motor to run all the time.

cooking appliances

THE INCREASING POPULARITY OF industrial cooking equipment has been a source of inspiration to manufacturers of residential cooking appliances. Today, these new appliances may incorporate bigger, hotter burners; more spacious ovens; built-in grills/griddles; and broilers with variable temperatures.

The first question you will want to answer before making a purchase is whether you prefer a range, which has both a cooktop and an oven, or separate wall oven and cooktop units.

ranges

A range is the traditional convenience center of the kitchen, putting all the basic cooking functions in one location. Ranges may be gas, electric, or a combination of the two.

A freestanding range is the most common choice and is usually the most eco-

This kitchen is a showcase of stainless-steel appliances: commercial/ residential gas range, side-by-side refrigerator, trash compactor, dishwasher, and range-top microwave.

nomical as well. A standard model is 30 inches wide with a cooktop above and an oven below; some models include a microwave/range hood at eye level. Typically, the backsplash includes a clock, timer, and/or controls.

A slide-in range fits snugly between cabinets. Flanges on either side cover the gap between the range and the countertop to allow for easy cleaning. The range has no backsplash, so the wall behind should be covered with a material resistant to heat and moisture.

A drop-in range fits into a cutout in a cabinet. Because it rests on top of the cabinet base, it lacks a slide-out storage drawer on the bottom. The top edge overlaps the counter surface, thus eliminating the troublesome space between the counter and the range.

Those who do a lot of cooking may be attracted to a commercial range, but there are several drawbacks: excessive weight, dangerous heat, and time-consuming cleaning requirements. Manufacturers have developed "commercial/residential" models better suited for home use. These offer the power, size, and distinctive stainless-steel finish of the commercial range without the drawbacks. However, they are relatively expensive.

A refurbished heirloom range from grandmother's day is charming but lacks such modern features as self-cleaning. Some new ranges mimic the old-style range, but they, too, are expensive.

An undercounter oven can fit neatly into an island or peninsula.

ELECTRIC COIL

The most economical of electric elements, coils are also the fastest to heat up. Dual-watt coils allow you to adjust heat to the size of the pan: Interior coils heat small pots; full rings heat large cookware.

SMOOTH-TOP ELECTRIC

These ranges have radiant ribbons or coil elements that lie beneath a ceramic-glass surface and deliver quick heat. The seamless surface of these cooktops allows for easy cleanup.

GAS WITH GRIDDLE

Gas burners lend themselves to more-controlled cooking methods such as quick sauté or wok cookery. Cooktops customized with a gas griddle include downdraft or backdraft ventilation.

COMMERCIAL-STYLE GAS

Residential/commercial or pro-style ovens have heavy-duty controls; sealed gas burners that deliver even, steady flames; and center grates that make it easy to shift pans for cooling.

wall ovens

A built-in oven can be mounted under the counter with a cooktop above but is more commonly placed higher on a wall. The great advantage of a wall oven is easy access: You don't have to crouch to get at baking goods. The standard width is 30 inches, but narrower models are available.

A double oven offers the possibility of roasting in one and baking in the other. Some people have both a range and a wall oven: Most everyday baking and broiling is done in the wall oven, and the range's oven is available for multicourse meals and large parties.

cooktops

A cooktop is basically the top of a range without the oven. It drops into a cutout in the counter, like a self-rimming sink, and slim models invade little of the cabinet space below. Most cooktops come in 30-

This streamlined, electric double oven almost looks like a section of cabinetry.

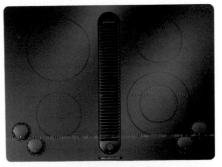

or 36-inch widths; they're all at least 2 to 3 inches shallower than the standard 24-inch cabinet depth.

Before installation, drop-in cooktops run from about 2½ to 8 inches high; figure about 16½ inches for downventing models. Both gas and electric cooktops include models that are "convertible"— they have modules that let you replace burners with grills, griddles, and other specialized accessories.

convection ovens

These are available in both gas and electric, freestanding or as part of a range. A convection oven has a high-speed fan that circulates the air, maintaining a steadier temperature. The result: Food cooks faster and browns evenly, meats are juicier, and baked goods have a more delicate texture. A "true" convection oven, with its burner in the rear of the oven chamber rather than at the bottom, works even better than a standard model.

heating options

It was once true that gas was the better choice for cooktops and electric the better choice for ovens. However, recent advances make both heat sources attractive options for either type of cooking. In most areas of the country, gas is more economical than electric power.

burners and grates

Choose burners to suit your pots and pans. Most people prefer one small burner, two that are medium-sized, and one

ABOVE LEFT: **A distinctively styled gas cooktop features four sealed burners as well as porcelain-on-cast-iron grates.** TOP RIGHT: **This frameless electric downdraft cooktop features a ceramic-glass surface, three single radiant elements, and one double.** ABOVE: **Gracing a solid-surface counter, this pro-style gas cooktop has downdraft ventilation along with high-output burners.**

cooking appliances

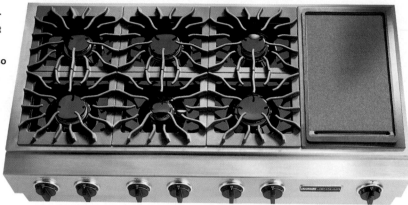

Six high-output gas burners will deliver rapid heat as well as delicate simmering temperatures. Also included is an electric nonstick griddle.

FEATURES TO LOOK FOR IN A RANGE, OVEN, OR COOKTOP

SELF-CLEANING This feature may add significantly to an oven's cost, but most people consider it well worth it. Two options are available. A continuous-cleaning oven has a special finish that continually oxidizes small amounts of spilled food whenever the oven is operating; it will not clean large spills, but wiping them away is easy. A regular self-cleaning oven heats up to 1,000° F and turns any food debris into a gray ash that can simply be wiped off.

WARMING DRAWER A pullout compartment with its own temperature control allows you to keep foods warm while you prepare other items.

STORAGE DRAWER Most freestanding ranges have a storage drawer. Look for one with a removable liner for easy cleaning.

BROILING FEATURES If you do a lot of broiling, buy a range with a broiler at the top so you don't have to crouch. Some models have only one broiling temperature, while others have variable temperatures.

CONTROLS Electronic controls offer a variety of features, including delayed start. Before making any purchase, test the controls to make sure you will be comfortable using them.

LOW-HEAT BURNER OPTION Both electric and gas burners on some units have controls that allow for very low heat, eliminating the need to cook certain foods in a double boiler or to use a heat diffuser.

RACKS An oven with three racks offers more possibilities than the standard two-rack oven. A half rack allows you to bake a tall item along with several shorter ones.

CHILD LOCKOUT This ensures that small children will not be able to open the oven door.

large burner for stock pots and the like. If you want more than four standard burners, the range or cooktop must be wider than 30 inches.

Some electric grates are designed so you can easily slide a pot from one to another. Some grill configurations include a central grate to rest pots for cooling.

Alternatives to the common burner include a central grill that allows you to barbecue indoors and a commercial-style griddle that provides a truly spacious cooking surface.

burner options

Gas is more flexible than ever, with both high- and low-volume BTU burners becoming standard features. A variety of attractive and easy-to-clean grate options are also commonly available. If you often use a wok or other round-bottomed pan, gas is the better choice. Choose sealed burners, which quickly wipe clean, and electric igniters rather than pilot lights.

Electric coils are the least costly and fastest to heat of the electric options. The more coils a burner has, the faster it heats up. Cleaning the coils, however, tends to be time-consuming.

Electric solid-disk (or solid-element) burners have a raised cast-iron surface that is textured so pans will not slip. They are easy to clean but can take a long time to heat up and cool down. Because they don't glow when hot, opt for a model with warning lights. These burners work best with heavy, flat-bottomed pans.

Smooth-top (or ceramic-glass) electric burners have become increasingly popular due to recent advances: They heat and cool quickly, and newer glass surfaces resist scratching. The burners glow when on, but it's still a good idea to buy a unit with a warning light that stays on until the burner is cool. One type has heating elements similar to standard heating coils, just under the glass surface.

Halogen bulbs also can be used underneath ceramic glass. They heat up quickly and glow red as soon as they're switched on. Once they are switched off, warning lights remain lit until the surface cools. They are energy-efficient but expensive.

Induction heat is another electric option for a ceramic-glass cooktop. Induction coils set up an electromagnetic field that reaches about an inch above the cooking surface. If you remove the pan, there's no live heat source; even at high heat, the surface feels cool to the touch. This option is expensive, and may not be readily available.

microwaves

Microwaves are especially popular for reheating leftovers, defrosting frozen foods, and cooking quick snacks like popcorn. Newer models come in an array of styles and colors. A microwave can simply be placed on a counter or table, but the more attractive option is to tuck it into a wall or above a cooktop. Many models are designed to be built right into the cabinetry. Standard-size models offer 1.5 cubic feet of cooking space and 1,000

Sensor functions for automatic popcorn, beverage, soup, and pizza preparation are offered in this stainless-steel microwave.

An above-range combination unit does double duty as a convection oven and a microwave.

watts of power, but larger and smaller models are available.

Older microwaves used so much power, they were required to have their own electrical circuit. Newer models do not use nearly as much power, but some local electrical codes still require that they be placed on a dedicated circuit.

cooktop **ventilation**

Properly installed, a range hood or downdraft ventilator will remove odors, smoke,

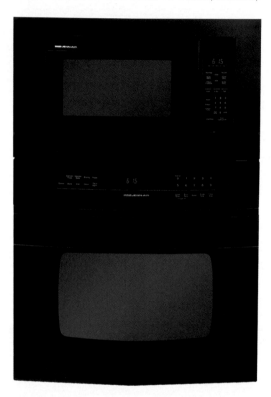

An efficient combination of microwave and oven is offered in a double unit. The microwave is 1,100 watts, and the bake/broil oven is dual-speed convection.

and heat from the kitchen. Only large-capacity commercial-style units will remove significant amounts of grease.

A ventilator will do little more than make noise if its blower is not powerful enough or the ductwork is inefficient. A cabinet-mounted range hood should pull 50 to 70 cubic feet per minute (CFM) for every square foot it covers. For example, a hood that is 36 inches by 24 inches covers 6 square feet; it should therefore be rated at 300 to 420 CFM. A freestanding hood should be rated at 100 CFM times the hood's square footage.

A ventilator is only as good as the duct to which it connects. If a duct is overlong, if it is made of ribbed rather than smooth ducting material, or if it takes more than a few turns, expect its drawing power to be compromised.

If running ductwork is difficult, consider installing a ductless hood. This draws air through a filter and sends it back into the kitchen. While not as efficient, it will lessen smoke and odors, which may be all you need.

To do its job properly, a range hood should cover the entire cooktop area plus at least 3 inches on either side. It should be positioned 24 to 30 inches above the cooktop—close enough to suck out smoke, steam, and odors but not so close as to interfere with the cooking process. Most range hoods are about 6 inches tall and have a funnel-shaped interior to feed fumes up to the filter and blower. Commercial units may locate the blower at the point where the duct exits the wall, making them much quieter than other units on the market.

A standard cabinet-mounted range hood is attached to the underside of the cabinet above the surface of the range. Most feature a light as well as the fan. If there is no cabinet above the range to hide the ductwork, consider installing a unit that's designed to be fully exposed. These tend to be large, relatively expensive—and a focal point of the kitchen.

FEATURES TO LOOK FOR IN A MICROWAVE

TURNTABLE A turntable rotates food for more-consistent heating. An inexpensive microwave without this feature will cook foods unevenly.

QUICK CONTROLS Some models calculate the time for you, so all you need do is press one or two buttons to defrost meat, cook a potato, heat a beverage, and so forth.

MELT-SOFTEN CYCLE Warm a stick of butter to just the right degree of softness with this feature.

CONVECTION/MICROWAVE OVEN You can combine the quick cooking time of a microwave with the browning and crisping capabilities of a convection oven.

LEFT: **Twice as quiet as the average vent, this range hood presents a low profile.** BELOW: **Stainless-steel design makes this hood both good-looking and easy-to-clean. Halogen lights provide illumination.**

downdraft ventilators Many commercial-style cooktops and ranges have downdraft ventilation systems. Some are located in the grillwork and draw smoke down into the center. Others (like the one shown above) rise up from the back of the cooktop and mount flush when not in use. These ventilators work nearly as well as range hoods, though they're not as effective at ventilating steam from tall pots.

kitchen lighting

EFFECTIVE LIGHTING MAKES A KITCHEN not only more functional but more pleasant. Ideally, a kitchen should be free of both shadows and glare. There should be medium-level light (ambient lighting) in most areas, as well as strong light over work areas (task lighting)—what kitchen designers call "layered lighting."

Build flexibility into your plan. Err on the side of too many rather than too few lights, and control them with separate switches. For additional control, include several dimmer switches.

Shiny surfaces reflect light and generally work well in a kitchen. High-gloss paint on cabinets, glossy counters, and glassy tiles make a kitchen bright and easy to clean. At eye level, however, too much light can create glare. The judicious use of satin paint or matte-finish tile will tone things down a bit.

ambient lighting

Start the planning process by deciding how the entire kitchen can be suffused with general illumination. A modest-sized kitchen may need only one source of ambient lighting, but adding another can have a stunning effect and highlight the kitchen's features.

Place a single large light in the center of the room. Then, if you choose to install recessed or track lights, run them around the ceiling's perimeter.

Ambient lighting should either be diffused or directed so that it bounces off a wall or ceiling. A fixture that points a spotlight directly downward will create shadows and inconsistent illumination. A diffusing globe or cover will spread out the light more evenly. Better yet, light that is pointed at the ceiling will provide large areas of a kitchen with gentle but effective lighting.

High ceilings are perfect for the formal touch of a chandelier.

Undercabinet lighting is an inexpensive solution to a dark kitchen. Fluorescent lights operate coolly and are very energy efficient. Low-voltage halogen lights are slim and can be dimmed.

One way to achieve subtle ambient lighting in a kitchen is to install cove lighting—a simple fluorescent or incandescent light placed on top of a wall cabinet or hidden behind a soffit. Cove lighting shines up at the ceiling all along one or more walls and can make a kitchen seem both taller and more spacious.

task lighting

Almost every kitchen needs undercabinet lighting. In standard kitchen design, the bottoms of wall cabinets are 54 inches above the floor and 18 inches above the countertop. Most adults standing at a countertop cannot see under the wall cabinet, making it the perfect place for task lighting. See the types available, at right.

Most cabinet-mounted range hoods include a diffused light that nicely illuminates the cooktop without glare. If you do not have a lighted range hood, carefully position one or two lights above the cook's head and near the wall in order to prevent shadows.

A kitchen sink is often placed in front of a window for pleasant lighting during the day. Add a recessed light or two for nighttime illumination.

The classic way to light up a dining area is with pendant lights or a modest chandelier. Position them with care so people won't bump their heads. If the light will shine downward, place it in the exact center of the table or counter to avoid creating shadows.

FROM TOP: Halogen spots let you place individual lights over a workspace. Line-voltage undercabinet halogen can be linked to others; its reflector can be tilted. Spot halogens in a light bar come with a built-in dimming capacity. Small fluorescent lights are not as sleek but are less costly and more energy efficient.

light fixtures

To provide proper illumination in a kitchen, you can choose from many different types and styles of light fixtures. Following is a closer look at some of the main options.

RECESSED DOWNLIGHTS (also called canister or pot lights) are popular choices for the kitchen. They are all but invisible and so will not conflict with any decor. Usually the trim is chosen separately from the canister itself. The most inexpensive trims result in an exposed light bulb that shines directly downward, producing shadows. Other trims surround the bulb with a baf-

fle to diffuse the light. Still other trims have a diffusing lens. Choose an IC (insulation-compatible) light if it will come near insulation or a combustible surface.

TRACK LIGHTING offers a great deal of flexibility. You can add, remove, or change around individual lights at will; a single track can hold several different lights so you have some for ambient lighting and others for task lighting. Track lights do need to be cleaned on a regular basis.

FLUSH-MOUNTED CEILING FIXTURES are often the least expensive. A modest incandescent fixture recedes visually almost as

This pendant light fixture with a frosted glass shade spreads soft, even light throughout the kitchen.

PENDANT

- Spreads light evenly
- Comes in all sorts of shapes and materials, including metal, glass, and paper
- Excellent light source over an island or dining table
- Incandescent and halogen

SCONCE

- Atmospheric light
- Available with multiple lights and in many styles and shapes
- Excellent for a breakfast nook or dining room
- Incandescent and halogen

FLUSH-MOUNTED

- Practical, strong light source, especially for a smaller kitchen
- Useful over a sink
- Can be very stylish or unobtrusive
- Incandescent, halogen, fluorescent

well as do canister lights. A large fluorescent fixture makes a kitchen very bright.

PENDANT FIXTURES add charm to a kitchen and provide effective task lighting. A pendant with a metal globe directs light downward in dramatic fashion, while a glass globe provides ambient as well as task lighting.

UNDERCABINET FIXTURES are available in many styles (see page 125).

SCONCE LIGHTS, mounted on the walls, come in many decorative styles; they provide both accent and ambient light.

CABLE LIGHTS hang like trapeze artists for a modern, European look. They are available in halogen form only, so be aware that they do get hot.

bulbs and tubes

Most kitchen lighting fixtures are fitted with either incandescent, halogen, or fluorescent bulbs or tubes.

Incandescent bulbs, the old standbys, are inexpensive but need to be replaced

fairly often and are not energy efficient. Compact fluorescents that can be screwed into an incandescent fixture are a better choice because they conserve energy and last far longer.

Fluorescent tubes produce bright light for a very small energy cost and do not get hot. Inexpensive fluorescent tubes, often used in offices and stores, may trigger headaches in some people. Newer tubes come in a range of tones, from cold to warm. "Full-spectrum" tubes mimic the sun's light.

Quartz halogen lights are very energy efficient and produce an intense, focused light. However, bulbs are expensive and can get very hot.

special switches

To enhance a lighting system's flexibility, place some lights on dimmer switches. A special switch is needed to dim a fluorescent fixture. To control a light fixture from switches at two different locations, you'll need to install three-way switches (see pages 192–193). Only one of the two switches can be a dimmer; the other must be a standard on-off switch.

windows and skylights

NATURAL SUNLIGHT MAKES A KITCHEN a warm, inviting place. While most people try to maximize cabinetry in their kitchens, you'll ultimately thank yourself for sacrificing a little storage space to make room for at least one large window.

When choosing a window, look for moving parts that operate smoothly and

An abundance of light floods into this kitchen through a combination of skylights and paned floor-to-ceiling windows.

gaskets and weather-stripping pieces that seal completely.

If possible, try to fit a standard-sized window into your plans since the price rises dramatically if the window must be custom-made.

window-framing materials

ALUMINUM Though older bare-aluminum windows were unattractive and poor insulators, newer units come with a tough anodized finish in attractive colors and often have a frame filled with plastic and foam insulation, making them more energy efficient. Painting certain aluminum windows may not be possible, so check with the dealer if this is your intention.

VINYL The least-expensive option, vinyl provides a high-quality window that is sturdy and a good insulator. However, it cannot be painted and colors may fade over time.

WOOD Attractive appearance, sturdy construction, and excellent insulating properties make wood a popular choice for windows. Wood needs to be protected from the elements with at least two good coats of paint or a stain and a clear finish, or it will rot. Some wood windows have visible "finger joints" where short lengths of wood have been spliced together end-to-end. These joints are visible if the windows are stained, so the windows must be painted. Some windows are available primed or even finish-painted. High-end

These casement
windows are bright,
offer unobstructed
views, and can be
clustered together for
architectural impact.

Though conventional
casement windows
hinge at one side, the
upper and lower sash of
this vinyl "horizontal"
casement drop down to
catch the breeze.

windows use solid pieces of wood. These
are beautiful if stained—just be aware that
wood windows are usually made from
softwood, which may be difficult to match
to hardwood cabinetry.

CLAD WOOD In this increasingly popular
option, all exposed parts are covered with
vinyl or aluminum that, in high-end windows, is extremely tough. Vinyl cladding
can be scratched, but the marks are generally not very evident because the color
goes all the way through.

window types

DOUBLE-HUNG This window has two sashes, both of which slide up and down and
are held open by weights, springs, or friction. The sash of a tilt-turn window disen-
gages at the top and tilts into the room to
ease cleaning the outside.

CASEMENT With this type of hinged window, a crank or lever swings the window
sash out or in. A casement window
"scoops" wind and directs it into a room
very effectively.

HORIZONTAL SLIDER With a slider, one or
both sashes move horizontally in a track,
so no mechanism is needed to hold a sash
open. Large varieties usually slide on
rollers. With most sliders, the sashes can
be easily removed for cleaning by lifting
them out of their tracks.

BAY This is typically composed of three
windows—any one of which may be
double-hung or fixed, and assembled so it
projects out from the wall.

GARDEN This can transform a sink area
into a small greenhouse. A garden window

is essentially a small bay window with glass above as well as on the sides. Vents provide for air flow.

glazing options

Glass is not a good insulator, but new glazing techniques help keep cold and heat out and can even maximize solar heat when you want it. Spending more for an energy-efficient window saves you money in the long run and makes your house more comfortable.

To judge a window's insulating ability, look for the R-value and the U-value. R-value indicates a glass's insulating properties—how well it prevents heat or cold from entering the house. U-value is a more comprehensive indicator telling you how much heat or cold flows through the entire window, including the frame. The lower the U-value, the more energy efficient the unit is.

Most windows today are double-glazed, meaning that they have two panes of glass sealed together; the space between is filled with gas, which insulates better than air. Triple-glazed windows offer even better insulation. Some high-end windows have operable blinds located between the panes; the obvious advantage to these kinds of units is that the blinds never need to be cleaned.

A window with low-emissivity (low-E) glazing has glass layered with a special film that screens out some unwanted solar rays but still lets in light. Low-E coatings keep heat from coming in or escaping and

Skylights set into a sloped ceiling transformed this dark, almost windowless kitchen (BELOW) into a bright, welcoming space (RIGHT).

Operable skylights are easy to open and close, thanks to a small motor concealed in the frame.

Natural light fills this airy kitchen from above. Several shading options are available for reducing heat and glare.

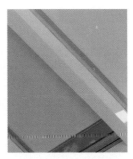

Light-block shades turn day into night. Made of fabric with exterior aluminum coating. Very energy efficient.

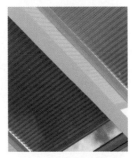

Pleated shades distribute soft filtered light, reducing glare and the fading effects of UV light on furnishings.

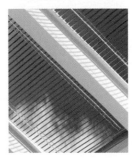

Venetian blinds offer optimal control over the direction and concentration of light. Easy to fit.

filter out ultraviolet rays, which can cause upholstery and other materials to fade.

Tinted glass, another option for skylights and some windows, is appropriate only if you want to minimize light. It also reduces the heat entering a room.

Obscure glass lets in some light but makes it impossible to see in or out. Several patterns are available; all have a frosted appearance.

"Smart" windows have a special glazing that senses temperature and light conditions and adjusts accordingly to shield out or let in sunlight. If possible, set a window like this in place temporarily, and test it for a day or two to see if you're satisfied with its performance.

Among high-tech window options are units that allow you to give a window a frosted look with the mere flip of a switch.

skylights

A skylight allows light in from above. One with clear glass focuses bright light on a small spot; a skylight with obscure glass or acrylic supplies more-general illumination.

A fixed skylight may be flat or dome-shaped. If installed correctly, it should seal out water reliably. Because window treatments for a skylight are impractical at best, you'll want to choose a unit with energy-efficient glazing.

For more money, you can buy a skylight that opens and closes. Some operate by hand crank, others are motorized, and still others operate automatically, opening when the air reaches a certain temperature. An open skylight can vent hot air and is compatible with air-conditioning since cold air stays near ground level.

Remote controls operate electric skylights; they can be programmed to open and close the skylights at a preset time.

window treatments

In this cheery kitchen, a yellow valance curtain and matching sink skirt soften and brighten the sink area.

NATURAL LIGHT SHINING INTO A kitchen is usually a welcome friend, so many people prefer the open, natural look of a window unadorned. But if your kitchen needs a little privacy or shade—or if your overall kitchen design needs a splash of color—then a window treatment may be just the thing. When selecting one, be aware that kitchen window treatments will need cleaning more often than those in other rooms.

curtains

Café curtains are a popular choice for kitchens. They cover the lower half of a window and usually mount inside the window frame where they're out of the way. A lightweight fabric will provide privacy while admitting light; sheer curtains diffuse light, producing partial privacy.

Tab-top curtains are a good choice where you want stationary curtains. They have cloth loops at the top instead of hardware to hold them in place; most do not glide easily—they're often used with tiebacks. The same is true for rod-pocket curtains, which also slide over the curtain rod without hardware.

shades, shutters, and blinds

Roller shades, the most common type, are now available in a wide choice of fabrics. The standard spring mechanism is the least expensive; a beaded-chain mechanism is more reliable.

Cellular shades, with a honeycomb-like design, let in highly diffused light. Various pleat sizes are available. This shade, while a fairly good insulator, is more easily damaged than other shade materials.

Woven shades may be made of bamboo, split wood, or natural reeds or fibers. Unlined shades let a little light filter

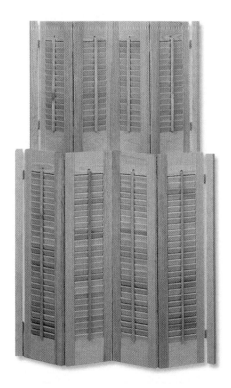

through. This type of shade may roll up or fold up; on a tall window, it may be quite thick when rolled up.

Roman shades, made in a variety of fabrics, have panels that draw up into neat, flat folds for a crisp, clean look.

London shades, also made of fabric, have cords at each side that are used to pull the fabric up so they have an attractive drape at the sides and bottom.

Window shadings are opaque slats that tilt like horizontal blinds, covered with sheer fabric. They offer maximum light and privacy control, as well as a stylish, contemporary ambience.

Decorative shutters, which attach to hinges on the inside of a window frame, are a particularly attractive choice for smaller windows. They may cover the entire window or just part of it (usually the lower half) for a café appearance.

Blinds come in a wide variety of materials and prices. Wood blinds with cloth ladder tapes have an appealing, traditional look. For smaller windows, micro-mini-blinds work well.

top treatments

Valances are basically a shortened version of curtains. Rod-pocket valances are especially popular in kitchens.

Cornices are made of wood that is either upholstered, painted, or stained. Like valances, they partner well with blinds or shades. The lower edge can either be curved or scalloped.

Swags and scarves are basically fabric artfully draped over a curtain rod. They lend an air of casual elegance and can be easily changed to suit your mood.

ABOVE LEFT: **Faux-wood mini-blinds easily adjust to bounce natural light into a room. They can be closed for privacy and to allow minimal light or be opened entirely for light and views.** ABOVE: **Hinged wooden shutters may cover the entire window or only part of it; like blinds, they adjust to control light and privacy.**

project workbook

REMODELING PRESENTS PLENTY OF CHALLENGES, FROM CULTIVATING IDEAS TO creating a floor plan to working with a building inspector. A bit of forethought can make the process go more smoothly—and that's where planning enters the picture. Planning a new kitchen is essentially a process of asking yourself the right questions and keeping track of your answers. No one knows better than you whether you have the need for a second dishwasher, the skill to install crown molding, or the stamina to prepare microwave dinners in the basement for a month. But these are the kinds of issues you must address when you launch into a kitchen remodeling project.

This chapter is a workbook, full of questions and checklists that can help you design your ideal kitchen and make your remodel as efficient, affordable, and painless as possible. You'll begin by considering your family's habits, preferences, and priorities. This is when you need to probe with such questions as "Can two territorial chefs share the cooking peninsula?" and "Will we tire of that cobalt blue cooktop?" Answers to questions like these, along with help from the information on the following pages, will provide the basis for creating the best kitchen for you. Then you'll be ready to take inventory of everything you need to get your project done, including securing financing, hiring and managing a professional designer or contractor, drafting contracts and agreements, dealing with building permits, and managing your project's progress.

Consider this workbook a starting point for your journey of self-inquiry. As you travel along, you'll discover other avenues to explore and roadblocks to negotiate. So exchange your rose-colored lenses for reading glasses and get ready to plot a course toward your destination: a beautiful new kitchen.

developing a plan

Choices, choices—it all begins with choices. This kitchen was given a monochromatic color scheme and central skylights to brighten it and create a sense of spaciousness.

YOU'LL PROBABLY EMBARK ON YOUR remodeling odyssey with at least a rough idea of how you want your new kitchen to look and how much money you want to spend. But how do you transform your vision into a workable strategy? Your practical side (not to mention various contractors and well-meaning relatives) may tell you to consider your finances first. But

that's a bit like planning your vacation based on how much you can spend rather than where you want to go. With cost as your starting point, you might get only as far as Paris, Texas, when a little creative thinking might have taken you to Paris, France. Your dream kitchen, like your dream vacation, may not include all the trappings you wanted originally. But if you start with a clear destination in mind, you're much likelier to end up on target.

decide what you like

First, envision your ideal kitchen, down to the last detail. A good place to start is the chapter that begins on page 10—it's packed with pictures of remodels and makeovers that may spark your imagination. After you've gathered a few ideas, expand your search. Visit the Lowe's website (www.lowes.com) for design and product ideas. Clip pictures from magazines and make a scrapbook of your kitchen hit parade. Check out remodels that your friends have done and look for features that appeal to you. Attend a home show. Take a neighborhood home tour. As you go about this process, pay close attention to your responses and note whether you are consistently attracted to certain motifs, materials, or layouts. In particular, focus on the following key design elements:

COLORS Consider whether you are drawn to warm, cheerful hues or to cool, soothing ones. Keep in mind that light tones and monochromatic color schemes can make a room seem more spacious, while dark colors can shorten a long, narrow space. You'll be living with your color

choices (except for painted surfaces) for a long time, so think about whether that purple laminate will pall over the years.

SURFACES Do you want the sleek, minimalist look of stainless-steel countertops? Does the warmth and pattern of a wood floor appeal to you? Choose rough textures to create an informal mood, smooth surfaces for elegance. Imagine how all your surfaces—from cabinets to appliances—will blend together.

SPACE Do you like your space to be defined, or prefer an open plan? Do you feel more comfortable in a cozy room or a ould an island seem convenient or confining? The size of your kitchen should determine the scale of your appliances, cabinets, and other large elements. To visually expand your space, include open shelves and plenty of windows, avoid extralarge appurtenances, and keep your overall design simple.

STYLE Is your taste traditional or contemporary? Do you want your kitchen to have a casual look or a polished one? What does the rest of your house look like? You don't need to slavishly mimic existing themes, but avoid mixing dramatically different styles. You probably won't want a Miami Moderne kitchen if your dining room's French Provincial.

be **practical**

Next you'll need to consider what kind of kitchen will really work for you and your family. Gather your family members together and discuss the following issues. Also, fill out the questionnaire on page 139, which will help your Lowe's Design Coordinator (or your contractor, if you hire one) to advise you.

USE How many cooks will be working at once? Will you need two sinks, extra counter space, or an oversized preparation island? Do you typically cook gourmet

meals for crowds of guests, or heat frozen dinners for two? Is a professional-quality range important? Two dishwashers? A convection oven? The Buyer's Guide that begins on page 76 can help you figure out what features to look for when choosing appliances and fixtures. Take advantage of the Lowe's website, or visit a Lowe's store to discuss your needs.

WEAR AND TEAR Do you have armies of people traipsing through your kitchen all day long? Are you a careful cook, or do you tend to set hot pans on the nearest available surface? Should you avoid materials that scratch, such as a marble countertop? Is your two-year-old (or your teenager) likely to assault the faucet handle? Consult the Buyer's Guide on page 76

This small-space kitchen glistens with stainless-steel appliances and sleek surfaces. Reflective materials fool the eye, making the space seem larger.

developing a plan

to research the durability of products you're considering.

EASE OF CLEANUP Are you keeping in mind that open shelves get dusty, glass cabinet doors can't hide clutter, grout gets grubby, and light colors show dirt? Be sure to evaluate ease of care and maintenance when considering various materials.

ACCESS How much storage do you need? Which equipment will require cabinet space and which will be stored in drawers? Will your kitchen need to accommodate a very short person, a very tall one, or someone with a physical disability?

THE ROOM Do you have enough space for the peninsula work center (or six-burner cooktop or double sink) you crave? Can you be satisfied making changes within your existing space, or will it be necessary to knock down walls to get the kitchen you want?

DISRUPTION How much upheaval can you tolerate? The bigger your project, the more it will encroach on your life. If you decide to add square footage, can you contend with the noise, dust, and inconvenience that attend a major remodel? (See page 152 for information on controlling disruption.)

list your **priorities**

You want your remodel to be fast, easy, inexpensive, and high quality. Often the best you can hope for is three out of the four. That's why it's crucial to identify what's really important to you. To do this, make a list that includes the following:

- What you absolutely must replace. If only half the burners on your stove work, deciding whether or not to buy a new one is a no-brainer. Replacing a perfectly good refrigerator with a new model is usually a lower priority.

- What you absolutely can't stand to keep. Your harvest-gold countertop may still be serviceable, but if you're sick to death of it, get a new one.

- What you absolutely can't live without. Will you kick yourself if you give up those custom cabinets? Will you still pine for a hardwood floor if you settle for a vinyl one?

put your plan **on paper**

Measure your kitchen using a tape measure. Your measurements should include the entire length of each wall, as well as the space between doorways, windows, and kitchen elements. Plot these distances on a sheet of drafting paper using one-half inch (two squares) to represent each foot of space. Note which direction your doors swing, where electrical fixtures and outlets are located, and anything else that might ultimately have impact on your new kitchen's design.

When you're ready to redesign your space, you can adopt this base map to create a new floor plan. Just leave intact the parts of your existing kitchen you intend to keep and sketch in the features you want to add.

Counter and cabinet heights and clearances are based on industry standards but can be altered to fit the cook or cooks—provided base cabinets and appliances will fit.

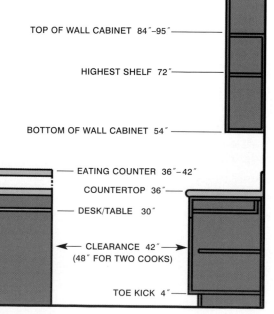

CEILING 96"

TOP OF WALL CABINET 84"–95"

HIGHEST SHELF 72"

BOTTOM OF WALL CABINET 54"

EATING COUNTER 36"–42"

COUNTERTOP 36"

DESK/TABLE 30"

STOOL 24"–32"

CLEARANCE 42" (48" FOR TWO COOKS)

TOE KICK 4"

Answer the questions below as thoughtfully and as thoroughly as you can. Your responses will help you and your Lowe's design coordinator tailor your new kitchen to your lifestyle, your family, and your wish list.

LIFESTYLE

How many people live in your household?

Adults _____ Teens _____ Children _____

Primary user(s):

Height _____ ☐ Right-handed ☐ Left-handed

Height _____ ☐ Right-handed ☐ Left-handed

KITCHEN USE

Our kitchen is to be:

☐ Remodeled ☐ New construction

Which meals do you prepare at home?

☐ Breakfast ☐ Lunch ☐ Dinner

What kind of food preparation do you do?

☐ Baking ☐ Canning ☐ Gourmet

☐ Microwave ☐ Other

What else is your kitchen used for?

Eating:

Table size _____ No. of chairs _____

No. of bar stools _____ Other _____

How many people eat at the same time? _____

Entertaining:

No. of people _____

Do guests help? _____

Leisure/hobby:

☐ Work-surface needs ☐ Homework

☐ Storage needs

Laundry:

☐ Full-size washer and dryer ☐ Stacked

☐ Folding space

Home office:

☐ Desk ☐ Storage ☐ Computer

Electronics:

☐ Television ☐ VCR/DVD ☐ Stereo

☐ Other

Special storage needs:

☐ Blender ☐ Breadmaker

☐ Cleaning supplies ☐ Coffeemaker

☐ Cookbooks ☐ Cutlery

☐ Fine china ☐ Food processor

☐ Glassware ☐ Linens

☐ Mixer ☐ Mops and brooms

☐ Pottery ☐ Recycling

☐ Sets of dishes ☐ Silverware

☐ Stemware ☐ Tableware

☐ Toaster ☐ Utensils

☐ Wok

Food storage needs:

☐ Canned goods ☐ Dry foods

☐ Pet foods ☐ Spices

Beverage storage needs:

☐ Cans ☐ Two-liter bottles

☐ Wine ☐ Other

EXISTING KITCHEN FEATURES

Cabinetry	☐ Keep	☐ Change
Colors	☐ Keep	☐ Change
Counter space and surface material	☐ Keep	☐ Change
Dining space	☐ Keep	☐ Change
Finish materials	☐ Keep	☐ Change
Flooring	☐ Keep	☐ Change
Layout	☐ Keep	☐ Change
Lighting	☐ Keep	☐ Change
Storage space	☐ Keep	☐ Change

NEW APPLIANCES/FIXTURES

Cooktop

Color/Material _____ Dimensions _____

Manufacturer _____ Model # _____

Dishwasher

Color/Material _____ Dimensions _____

Manufacturer _____ Model # _____

Faucet

Color/Material _____ Dimensions _____

Manufacturer _____ Model # _____

Microwave oven

Color/Material _____ Dimensions _____

Manufacturer _____ Model # _____

Oven(s)

Color/Material _____ Dimensions _____

Manufacturer _____ Model # _____

Range

Color/Material _____ Dimensions _____

Manufacturer _____ Model # _____

Range hood

Color/Material _____ Dimensions _____

Manufacturer _____ Model # _____

Refrigerator

Color/Material _____ Dimensions _____

Manufacturer _____ Model # _____

Sink

Color/Material _____ Dimensions _____

Manufacturer _____ Model # _____

paying for your kitchen

New paint, lighting, and surfaces, when coupled with a few choice details like this kitchen's pot rack and chopping block, can give a kitchen an entirely fresh sense of charm and style.

FOCUS ON REMODELING ECONOMICS. First decide whether you'll get a reasonable return on the investment you're making in your house. Then read on for suggestions about setting a budget, obtaining financing, and controlling costs.

return on **investment**

In most cases, it makes good financial sense to update your kitchen. Provided that you intend to stay in your house for at least a year, you can often recoup most of your remodeling costs when you sell, and in some markets you'll get back even more than you spent on a new kitchen. No matter where you live, a simple kitchen facelift (new paint, countertops, fixtures, and flooring) is the most profitable home improvement you can make. But be cautious: You're unlikely to be rewarded for creating a kitchen that's far grander than the others on your block,

since buyers usually won't pay more than a 10 to 15 percent premium for a house that's better than its neighbors. Of course, if you know you'll be staying in your house for a long time, or you simply want your dream kitchen regardless of whether the next buyer will value it, then you can forge ahead and forget about this part of the planning process.

your **ideal** kitchen's cost

Asking how much it costs to remodel a kitchen is like asking how big a dog is. If you have a Chihuahua-sized remodel in mind, your expenses may be modest; a St. Bernard–sized overhaul could easily set you back six figures.

The surest way to send your remodeling bill into the stratosphere is to make structural changes to your kitchen. If you build an addition, move a bearing wall, alter a ceiling or roofline, or install windows, skylights, or even a heavy floor, you may need to make expensive structural modifications. Unless you have the expertise to do much of this work yourself, have your checkbook ready and your pen poised.

If you're able to work within the space you have, cabinets will be your biggest expense. As the chart at right shows, new cabinets typically account for a major chunk of the cost of a new kitchen, so it makes sense to begin by figuring out how much you'll pay for them. Revisit your planning questionnaire (page 139) and your floor plan, and consult the Buyer's Guide on page 76 to see what features you'd like. Then go to a Lowe's store (or to www.lowes.com) to compare your options; Lowe's has a vast array of cabinets in every price range. Have your base map with specific measurements handy so you can accurately estimate your cost. Follow the same procedure for your other big-ticket items—countertops, flooring, and appliances—and your budget will be nearly complete. Labor will typically add another 15 percent or more, but of course

CABINETS 48%

LABOR 16%

COUNTERTOPS 13%

APPLIANCES 8%

DESIGN SERVICES/MISCELLANEOUS 7%

FLOORING 4%

FIXTURES AND FITTINGS 4%

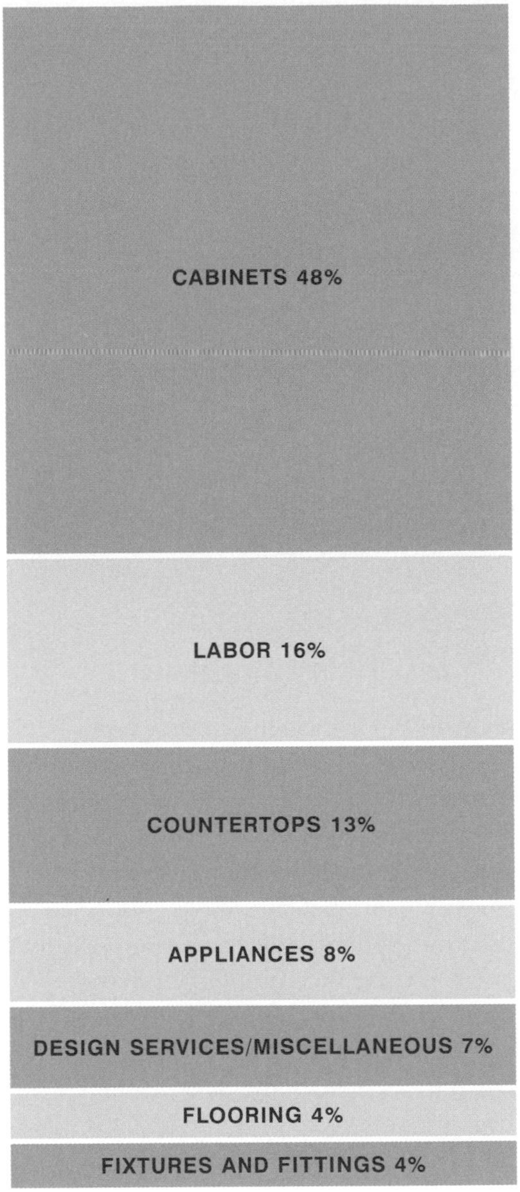

Though average costs of kitchen improvements can vary dramatically, depending on the nature of the work being done, this chart illustrates how kitchen components and services typically weigh in on a relative scale. Note that cabinets account for nearly half of the typical kitchen remodeling budget.

you won't have that expense if you're doing the work yourself.

cutting costs

If the projected bill for your dream kitchen gives you nightmares, review your biggest expenses (it may help to make a chart like the one above). Ask yourself how extensive a remodel you really need. If you're planning structural changes, decide whether you can work with your existing space instead. Think about whether you can get the effect you want with a few cosmetic improvements rather than a major renovation.

You can also make significant cuts to the bottom line by revising your plans for

paying for your kitchen

When it's time to work out your budget or choose an improvement loan, you'll need to do a little homework.

cabinets, appliances, and other major design elements. Go back to your list of priorities, then scan your budget for anything that didn't seem crucial to you at the start of the planning process. Is there a costly item you can live without or an existing appliance you can keep? Perhaps you can make do with off-the-shelf cabinets instead of built-to-order ones, or choose a mid-price line instead of high-end models. Check the Buyer's Guide, beginning on page 76, and talk with a Lowe's Design Coordinator to see what tradeoffs you can make. One practical way to lower your costs is to step down from state-of-the-art appliances to more basic ones; perhaps you don't really need the extra features that invariably drive up the cost. Check out less-expensive materials for countertops and flooring; creative use of vinyl flooring, laminates, and other moderately priced surfaces can result in a fabulous look.

Since labor can account for nearly a fifth of the cost of a kitchen remodel, you can save a lot of money by finding someone who will work for free—that would be you. There are many simple jobs that even an amateur handyperson can handle. Take a look at the Do-It-Yourself Guide

that begins on page 156 for step-by-step instructions on how to perform basic remodeling tasks. You can also find helpful people at Lowe's to advise you on installing products. But be realistic: The fact that you can install a faucet doesn't mean that you should necessarily jump into replacing your sink, counters, and cabinets by yourself.

figuring out **finances**

Suppose your new kitchen's estimated cost exceeds your checking account balance by a factor of ten. Don't be tempted to finance your project with plastic: Credit card interest rates are high, and you can't deduct the interest from your taxes. Instead, check into getting a loan. Several options for borrowing money are available, and most are tax-deductible. Here are your basic choices:

REFINANCE You can get a new mortgage on your house, taking a larger loan than you had before. Lenders will usually determine the loan amount by figuring out what your house will be worth after you remodel it. You'll start over with a new interest rate and, in most cases, you'll pay points and closing costs just as you would on any mortgage.

HOME-EQUITY LOAN You can borrow against the equity you have in your house—that is, the difference between what your house is worth and the amount you owe on your mortgage. You may pay a higher interest rate than you would on a refinance, but closing costs are generally lower. Ask the bank to compare up-front expenses and monthly payments.

HOME-IMPROVEMENT LOAN This may be your only option if you have little or no equity in your home. There are several types of home-improvement loans, all secured with the future value of your house. As with home-equity loans and mortgages, the interest is tax-deductible.

hiring professionals

MAYBE THE SCOPE OF YOUR PROJECT exceeds your skill level, or maybe you'd simply prefer not to have paint specks on your watch and drywall dust in your hair for weeks on end. Whatever the reason, you're bound to want professional help at some point during your remodel. If you can handle everything but the major jobs—moving a supporting wall or updating your electrical service, for example— you may need only a subcontractor or two. If you're handier with a putter than a paintbrush, you might decide to deploy a platoon of professionals. No matter what your experience (or lack thereof), you can do quite a bit of work yourself if you have the time and the determination, since many remodeling tasks are relatively simple and straightforward (see the Do-It-Yourself Guide that begins on page 156). If you do choose to fly solo, Lowe's has experts on staff to advise you, and each store offers classes to give you hands-on experience in everything from setting tile to painting. If you plan to hire a professional, be sure to find one whose skills match your needs:

ARCHITECTS Architects can handle a remodel from soup to nuts: They'll design a functional, attractive space, get bids from general contractors, and supervise the actual work. They're also able to make calculations for structural changes; other professionals aren't allowed to make such changes unless a state-licensed engineer designs the structure and signs the working drawings.

GENERAL CONTRACTORS General contractors specialize in construction, but the job description can vary. Some contractors handle all the work themselves, while oth-

ers do nothing but schedule and supervise subcontractors. Some will offer design services, while others will require you to provide a professional-quality plan. A contractor is the professional to hire if you don't relish managing people or focusing on minute details.

SUBCONTRACTORS Subcontractors such as plumbers, electricians, and carpenters specialize in a particular aspect of construction. You can hire subcontractors on your own, which means that you'll be acting as your own general contractor. With this type of arrangement, you can do some of the work yourself or subcontract all of it.

Do it yourself? Definitely not! If your kitchen remodel involves elaborate design, high-level craftsmanship, and materials that are tricky to work with, call in professionals for help.

Whether or not you're an avid do-it-yourselfer, leave heavy, awkward, dangerous work in the hands of a qualified contractor—and structural design and planning to an architect or engineer.

LOWE'S CAN DO IT
Here are just a few of the items that Lowe's licensed professionals can install in your kitchen:

- Cabinets
- Countertops
- Dishwashers
- Flooring
- Garbage disposals
- Hot-water dispensers
- Interior and exterior doors
- Lighting and ceiling fans
- Ranges
- Replacement faucets
- Windows
- Window treatments

LOWE'S SERVICES When you shop at Lowe's, you can arrange for installation services while you're making a purchase. All work is done by licensed professionals and fully guaranteed by Lowe's. Just tell your sales associate which items you'd like to have installed, and pay for the items and installation services at the same time. An installer will call you to arrange an appointment, and the work will be done efficiently and neatly at a time that's convenient for you. Lowe's guarantees that you'll be completely satisfied with the results. Please note that Lowe's installation services do not include plumbing or hard wiring. To find out more about how Lowe's professional installers can help with your kitchen remodel, visit your Lowe's store, or call 1-877-GO LOWES.

KITCHEN DESIGNERS Kitchen designers can help you come up with an entire kitchen plan, not to mention tell you about the latest trends and techniques. If you decide to hire one, look for a Certified Kitchen Designer (CKD) or a member of the National Kitchen & Bath Association (NKBA).

INTERIOR DESIGNERS Interior designers focus on decorating and furnishing a room. Their finishing touches can add polish to a remodel, and they have access to materials and products not available at the retail level.

do you **need a pro?**
Deciding whether to hire a professional is one of the most crucial choices you'll make when planning your new kitchen. You can save money by doing the work yourself, but only if you're up to the task.

Be aware that performing as a contractor is a real job. It involves ordering your own materials and keeping detailed records of purchases and deliveries, as well as finding qualified subcontractors who will work at reasonable prices, learning about local building codes and obtaining permits, dealing with inspectors, and handling insurance and possibly even payroll taxes.

Before stepping into this role, consider the following:

Do you have the skills? Neophytes can tackle most of the jobs described in the Do-It-Yourself Guide that begins on page 156. Whether you should undertake more-complicated projects depends on several things, including the extent of the work, your skills, your available time, and your collection of tools.

In regard to structural changes, the law usually requires that you enlist a licensed architect or engineer to create a structurally sound design.

Consider how visible the results will be. The more permanent and prominent the improvement, the more you'll need professional-quality work. Save skill development for places not readily seen.

Think about safety. Make sure you won't be endangering yourself or your family when you work with electricity, gas, dangerous tools, or heavy loads—or on precarious perches.

Factor in your time. Contracting your own home improvement on a part-time basis can extend the life of the project considerably; if speed is a priority, call in a pro. If you do decide to go it alone, keep in mind that most people underestimate how long a job will take. To be on the safe side, double the amount of time you think you'll need. You'll also want to allow extra time to repair mistakes caused by inexperience. Don't neglect putting a value on your time, and consider whether the money you'll save is really worth the time you'll spend.

Do you have the tools? A major kitchen remodel can require an arsenal of tools. Of course, you can buy new tools or rent specialized equipment (the tile saw shown at right, for example). But remember that buying and renting tools will add to the bottom line. If the cost of obtaining tools adds significantly to your do-it-yourself budget, a professional's bid might seem more agreeable.

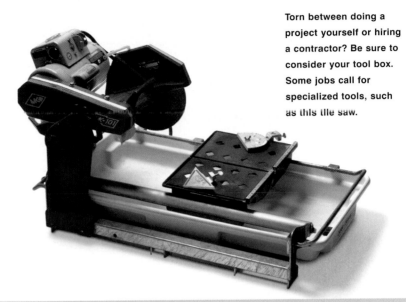

Torn between doing a project yourself or hiring a contractor? Be sure to consider your tool box. Some jobs call for specialized tools, such as this tile saw.

FINDING A QUALIFIED PROFESSIONAL

A skilled professional can be an invaluable ally when remodeling your kitchen. It's important to find someone with a proven track record and a personality you find palatable. Here are some steps you can take to find a pro who meets your needs:

■ Ask friends for recommendations. If you're already working with a professional you like, ask him or her to recommend specialists in other aspects of kitchen remodeling. Your Lowe's store also offers a wide variety of remodeling and installation services.

■ After you have gathered some names, interview several professionals with experience working on projects like yours (for a big job, talk to at least three).

■ Request written, itemized bids that include a breakdown of time, materials costs, and labor rates. Will the work be guaranteed and, if so, for how long?

■ Don't ignore your gut reaction. You're beginning a relationship with someone who will be in your house every day. If you feel uncomfortable, even if you can't pinpoint the reason, keep looking.

■ Request names of satisfied clients from the professionals you are considering. When you contact a former client, ask these important questions: 1) Was the project completed as promised and on time? 2) Was the person prompt, reliable, and tidy? 3) Did (s)he deal effectively with other profession-

als on the job? 4) Was (s)he easy to work with and pleasant to have around?

■ Ask to see the finished work. Most design and construction professionals can supply photographs of the projects they've completed, and some will even arrange for you to visit former clients' homes.

■ Ask about logistics. Will the person you're hiring do the work or supervise others? Will (s)he be working on other jobs at the same time as yours? How long will the job take? When will work begin?

■ Make sure your candidates have appropriate credentials. General contractors should be licensed and bonded; your state contractors' board can provide information about current licensees and any complaints lodged against them. Architects are licensed by the state as well. Many professionals also belong to organizations such as the American Institute of Architects, the National Kitchen & Bath Association, or the American Society of Interior Designers.

■ Talk about money. Will you receive a firm bid, or will you be expected to pay for the person's time and the cost of materials? If the deal is for time and materials, will an estimate include a "not to exceed" figure?

■ Inquire about each person's status with the Better Business Bureau (703-276-0100 or www.bbb.org).

plans and contracts

THE FIRST THING YOU NEED TO KNOW about a contract is that you should have one. Even when you're confident you've found trustworthy, skilled professionals, it's important to get everything in writing. A written agreement helps prevent misunderstandings and disagreements and serves as a backup if a dispute should arise between you and your contractor.

what it should **include**

A contract is a legal agreement that obligates the people who sign it to perform specific acts. Note the word "specific." Make sure any contract you sign spells out exactly what you expect from any professional you hire. Here are some elements you should include:

Written contracts are a critical part of any project that involves hiring a professional.

- Start and finish dates. You may want to include the phrase "time is of the

essence," which may give you added leverage if a delay leads to a dispute.

- The right to settle disputes by arbitration. In the event of a dispute, arbitration can often be speedier and less costly than a court proceeding.

- A warranty of at least a year on all work and materials. Some states require a contractor to warranty his or her work for at least five years (ten years for hidden problems).

- A payment schedule. Never pay more than 10 percent or $1,000, whichever is lower, up-front. Pay as the work progresses in order to provide continual incentives for completing work and to protect yourself from a contractor who might disappear with your money. The final payment should be made only upon satisfactory completion of the job. If speed is important, you may want to include a late-penalty clause and/or a bonus for early completion.

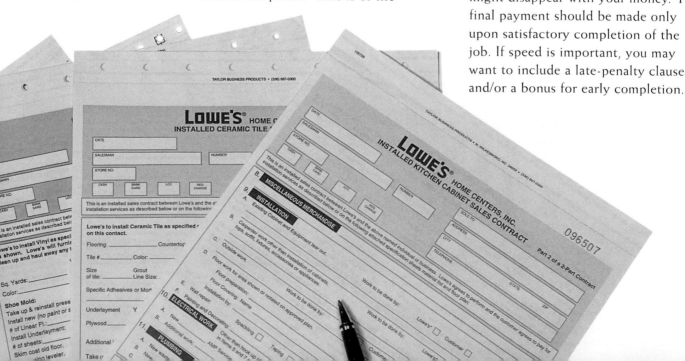

- Detailed job and materials descriptions. Be sure of the choices before you draw up the contract, then spell these out in it. If you want flooring made of 3-inch-wide No. 1 maple, put it in writing. Be sure that contractual allowances will cover the cabinets, fixtures, appliances, and materials you want.

- A waiver of subcontractor liens. In some states, subcontractors can place a lien on your property if the general contractor fails to pay them. To protect yourself from this consequence, specify that final payment will not be made until the contractor gives you an unconditional release of these rights from all subcontractors and suppliers who provided services or materials.

- If amendments or "change orders" are made along the way, make sure that both parties initial them.

avoiding conflicts

A contract will help you establish productive relationships with the professionals you hire, but it's no guarantee that your remodel will go smoothly. A piece of paper cannot substitute for basic courtesy and common sense.

Use this book to educate yourself about the fundamentals of kitchen remodeling so you'll understand what the professional is proposing and why.

Before you sign a contract, study it to verify that you and the professional have the same understanding of what will be done. Check your research to be sure that contractual price caps will cover the costs of the kitchen elements you want.

When professionals arrive at the job site, respect their skills. It's fine to ask questions and keep tabs on the progress of your project, but don't niggle or pester.

By all means be polite, but do speak up promptly if you have a concern. It will be much more difficult to make a change once the job is finished.

HANDLING CONTRACTOR PROBLEMS

If you're unhappy with the way your contractor is handling your remodel, your first step should be simply to express your concerns in person. Most contractors will make every effort to ensure that you're satisfied with their work. Should you reach an impasse, an architect, designer, or other professional who knows your project may be able to help broker an agreement. If such personal approaches don't work, you can take one or more of the following actions, beginning with the least drastic measure:

1 Send a certified letter outlining the contract requirements you consider to be unfulfilled and stipulating a reasonable time frame for compliance. Sometimes this is enough to inspire action.

2 File a complaint with the Better Business Bureau (BBB) at 703-276-0100 or www.bbb.org. The BBB will forward your complaint to the contractor, who may consider your requests in order to avoid an unfavorable BBB report.

3 Contact the local or state board that licenses contractors, if one exists in your area. Contractors have a strong incentive to maintain a clean record with the licensing board, since some boards have the power to levy a fine or even revoke a license in cases of serious negligence or incompetence.

4 If both parties agree, try to resolve the dispute informally through a mediator. The BBB and many local organizations offer mediation services to help businesses and consumers work out mutually agreeable solutions.

5 Present your case before an impartial arbitrator. More formal than mediation, but much less costly and time-consuming than litigation, arbitration gives both parties the opportunity to present evidence in a joint hearing. The arbitrator's decision is usually binding. You can arrange arbitration through the Better Business Bureau, or through the American Arbitration Association (www.adr.org).

6 If you're seeking minimal damages (the amount varies from state to state but is usually no more than a few thousand dollars), bring your case to small claims court. You won't need an attorney, and court costs are usually modest.

7 If you're suing for a large amount of money, you can file a civil suit. This option has definite drawbacks: The case may drag on for months or even years, and your costs can exceed any award you may receive. Remember that if you have fired a contractor who has essentially done the work as agreed, you are the one who will be found to have breached the contract. Make every effort then, when drawing up a contract, to be explicit about the work to be done.

codes and permits

IF YOU'RE PERFORMING MINOR cosmetic surgery on your kitchen, you probably won't have to worry about building codes and ordinances. However, if you're making changes to your kitchen's structure, plumbing, or electrical wiring, you'll need to obtain permits from your city or county building department before you can begin your project. You may also be required to submit detailed drawings of the changes you plan to make. During construction, the building department will send inspectors at several points to verify that the work has been done satisfactorily (usually, it is up to you to call to schedule the inspections).

If you're working with an architect or a general contractor, this professional will handle permits and inspections. Each is familiar with local building codes and can be enormously helpful in getting plans approved, obtaining variances, and passing inspections.

Keep an approved set of your building plans at the job site so building officials can refer to them during inspections.

your to-do list

Here's a to-do list if you decide to act as your own general contractor:

- Check with your building department if you're putting on an addition. Local codes usually specify how far from the property line a house must be. If your addition will be too close, you may need a variance, or you may be prohibited from building at all.

- Find out whether you'll need to submit your plans for approval.

- Ask whether the building department can send you printed information about the ordinances that apply to your remodel and the various types of permits you'll need.

- If you're a diehard do-it-yourselfer, be aware that in some regions only certified electricians or plumbers are legally allowed to install or upgrade wiring and pipes.

- Prepare for inspections. Read pertinent sections of the building code so you'll know exactly what the inspector will be looking for (see "Inspections" at right). If you hire subcontractors, they may agree to be present when their work is inspected.

the purpose of a permit

A permit protects the homeowner. If a professional suggests that you don't need one, check with the building department yourself: You probably do, and it's to your advantage to get one. In fact, this suggestion is usually a red flag that your contractor is trying to cut corners to your detriment. In most cases, you'll pay a fee based on the value of the project (don't overestimate the value of your work, or you'll pay more).

A permit ensures oversight of your contractor's work (or yours). The scrutiny of an inspector can guard against mistakes and shoddy workmanship and give you assurance that the work adheres to building codes. You'll sleep better knowing that your project meets safety standards for materials and construction techniques.

It will also help you avoid headaches in the future. If building officials discover that you've done work without a permit, you could be required to dismantle your remodel and start over again. If you sell your house, you may be legally obligated to disclose that you've remodeled without a permit, and the buyer could demand that you bring the work up to code.

inspections

When you obtain a permit for your kitchen remodel, your building department can tell you what inspections you'll need and when they should be done. Some tasks require more than one inspection. Electrical work, for example, is inspected when circuits are roughed in, again when changes to the electrical service are completed, and finally when all appliances and devices have been installed,

grounded, and energized. Inspectors will look for the following things when they visit your worksite:

- A copy of the building permit, posted where it can easily be seen.

- A record of all inspections that have been completed, with inspectors' signatures included.

- Proof that mechanical equipment such as wiring and pipes were installed by certified professionals, if such requirements exist in your area.

- Compliance with local codes, including safety and zoning issues. Obtain copies of all relevant ordinances from your local building department.

Altering the roofline, changing the house's structure, moving or replacing plumbing fixtures or electrical wiring: These are just a few of the jobs that call for a building permit—and are best left to professionals unless you are very skilled.

WHEN DO YOU NEED A PERMIT?

You probably need a permit if you plan to . . .
- Change the footprint of your house by adding space to your kitchen
- Move a load-bearing wall
- Alter the roofline
- Create a new door or window opening
- Replace an electric stove with a natural-gas model
- Move a sink
- Replace plumbing fixtures

But not if you plan to . . .
- Install new floor coverings
- Replace doors or windows without altering the structure
- Change a countertop
- Replace a faucet

project management

A MAJOR KITCHEN REMODEL TAKES at least two months even if all goes well. When you put your kitchen out of commission for that long, you have to endure a certain amount of upheaval. But there are some simple steps you can take to make the ordeal a bit more bearable.

First, plan the progress of your remodel carefully: You don't want to gut your kitchen six weeks before your cabinets arrive or pour the foundation for an addition that violates local ordinances. The

planning
ONE MONTH OR MORE

■ Order cabinets and appliances.

■ Clean out the garage, basement, or other area of your home where you plan to store the contents of your kitchen during remodeling.

■ Inspect cabinets and appliances as they arrive. Make sure that the delivery person waits to see if any returns will be necessary. If your purchase came from Lowe's, report any problems; Lowe's stands behind every product it sells.

■ Rent a dumpster for demolition debris, as well as a portable toilet for construction workers if you'd rather they not use your bathroom.

■ Set up an alternate kitchen in the dining room, basement, or other area. Move in a hotplate, microwave, small refrigerator, and a few dishes.

■ Pack up and move your kitchen equipment.

■ Get rid of old appliances. Sell them or donate to charity.

demolition
TWO TO THREE DAYS

■ Cover kitchen doorways with heavy sheets of clear plastic to contain dust and debris.

■ Shut off electricity, then water.

■ Remove sink.

■ Remove countertop.

■ Remove and salvage base cabinets, then upper cabinets.

■ Handle any structural demolition.

timeline here will help you complete your project as quickly as possible with a minimum of costly interruptions. If you hire subcontractors, follow the schedule at right ("Sequencing Trades") to make sure that each one arrives at the right point in the process.

During construction, a few precautions will mitigate the effects of remodeling on your family and your possessions.

before you begin . . .

Get a permit from your local building department. Do not proceed until your project gets the go-ahead; you could be wasting time and money. Order custommade items such as windows, doors, and

SEQUENCING TRADES

If you're acting as your own general contractor, one of your most important tasks is scheduling the subcontractors. Errors in scheduling can be costly and inconvenient. Ask your subcontractors how long each step of your project will take, then schedule their arrival in the following order:

1. Rough carpenters
2. Heating and air-conditioning contractor
3. Plumber (rough plumbing)
4. Electrician (rough wiring)
5. Drywall contractor
6. Cabinetmaker or installer
7. Countertop installer
8. Plumber (finish work)
9. Electrician (finish work)
10. Flooring contractor
11. Finish carpenter
12. Painter

construction
FOUR TO FIVE WEEKS

- Do all rough construction work and any installation of doors and windows.

- Install ductwork for heating and air-conditioning.

- Update electrical service if necessary, and install rough wiring for outlets, switches, lighting, and appliances.

- Route water lines as well as drainage pipes for sinks and appliances requiring a water source.

- Hang and finish drywall.

finishing
FOUR TO FIVE WEEKS

- Install cabinets, including doors and hardware.

- Install countertops. Allow less than a week for laminate, a month or more for solid surfaces such as granite.

- Install sinks and faucets.

- Install lighting, switches, and receptacles.

- Install underlayment for flooring, if needed. If you've chosen sheet vinyl, install it at this point and cover it carefully to protect it during ongoing construction.

- Install flooring. Allow a day or so for vinyl squares, two days for hardwood, up to a week for tile or stone.

- Install trim.

- Prime and paint walls and trim.

- Install appliances.

- Install electrical and lighting cover plates and trims.

project management

Be prepared for dust, and plenty of it! Keep lots of duct tape and plastic sheeting on hand for sealing up doorways to isolate work areas.

controlling **disasters**

Even when everything goes smoothly, a kitchen remodel can be trying; when things go wrong, it can be downright traumatic. You can minimize irritations and prevent calamities by taking a few simple precautions:

- Plan carefully. It's a grievous and unnecessary inconvenience to live with a hole in an exterior wall while you're waiting for the out-of-stock window you should have ordered earlier.

- Time the work to avoid inclement weather and major holidays. If you're planning to have Christmas dinner at your house, for example, you're pushing your luck to start your remodel in October; you'll want to avoid having to work under an inflexible deadline. Also, don't expect much work to happen over the holidays.

- Don't go on vacation. Even if you have a general contractor, you'll need to make decisions and keep an eye on the progress of your remodel.

- Do arrange to be out of the house for a short time when there will be unbearable noise, noxious fumes, or any other threats to your health or well-being.

- Get phone numbers for the key people who will be working on your project, and ask the general contractor for a home number and/or cell phone number. Make sure that every tradesperson knows how to reach you. If you haven't got a cell phone, consider getting one.

- Plan strategies for feeding your family. Set up a temporary kitchen, and don't forget to arm yourself with an arsenal of takeout menus.

- Establish and post a set of house rules regarding the use of phones and bathrooms, keeping pets indoors or out, and similar issues.

- Seal interior doorways with plastic sheeting and duct tape to keep out dust, especially when you sand drywall.

- Be mindful of home security. Remember that you'll have hordes of strangers in your house. Be careful about giving out keys and burglar-alarm combinations. Don't leave valuables unattended.

remodeling **safely**

Above all, you want to emerge from your remodel in one piece—with your house intact and your family in good health. Remodeling can be a dangerous business, and careless work habits can cause disasters and even death. Talk with your insurance agent about the coverage you should maintain during your remodel, and be sure your contractor is covered for liability and worker's compensation. Be on the lookout for potential hazards whenever you're on the job, and take these precautions:

■ Keep the work area well lit and uncluttered. Plan your setup before you begin. Clean up as you go, removing debris that might cause uncertain footing. Don't leave tools lying around.

■ Wear appropriate clothing including long pants and sturdy shoes or workboots, as well as safety gear (see below). Never wear loose-fitting clothing that could catch in a tool's mechanism; tie back long hair.

■ Keep the area very well ventilated when you're using finishes or chemicals that give off fumes.

■ Use only power tools that are double-insulated or grounded. If you're working in a damp area, be sure you plug into an outlet protected by a ground fault circuit interrupter (GFCI or GFI; see page 191).

■ Keep tools in good working order. Make sure that blades and bits are sharp and that safety devices such as guards are undamaged.

■ Don't lift loads that are too heavy, and bend at the knees when you pick up large items. Work with a partner when you need help, but avoid working with another person in tight places where you might injure one another.

■ Don't work when you're tired. You're most likely to be injured while cutting "just one more" tile or 2 by 4.

■ Shut off power in the service panel before you begin any electrical work or open up walls where wiring may be present. Be sure you know which circuit breakers control which circuits. Use a neon tester to double-check that the circuit is off. Working with electricity is one of the riskiest jobs you can undertake. If you're not sure you can handle a task, call in a professional.

YOU SHOULD HAVE ON HAND:

SAFETY GLASSES Protect your eyes when using power tools or tools that involve striking an object (a hammer and chisel, for example).

HARD HAT Wear one if you will be working with a partner in a cramped space or if falling objects could hit you.

EAR PROTECTORS Use these when you will be working with noisy machinery.

DUST MASK OR RESPIRATOR Be sure that a respirator is approved for filtering the pollutants you are handling, including dust, fibers, and harmful vapors. A dust mask like the one shown is helpful when working around common dust.

GLOVES Choose leather to protect your hands from scratches and splinters, rubber when handling caustic chemicals.

kitchen safety

BECAUSE THE KITCHEN IS FILLED WITH machines, sharp utensils, and activity, it is one of a home's most dangerous rooms. Given this, it's wise to consider safety issues when planning a remodel or new construction, particularly if the household includes young children or elderly people. Following are a few important steps you can take to minimize hazards, making your new kitchen safer for everyone.

Positioning the range away from kitchen hub-bub and installing effective ventilation help make a safe kitchen.

planning for safety

Be sure all work is done according to building codes and inspected by building officials. This will ensure that all gas lines, plumbing, wiring, and general construction meet minimum standards and are safe.

Incorporate safety solutions into your kitchen layout and traffic patterns. Provide clear pathways for carrying just-cooked food to the dining area, and instead of installing a swinging door, opt for a pocket door into the kitchen. Be sure an open door on a cabinet, microwave, dishwasher, or oven won't suddenly become a hazardous obstacle.

Locate the range away from windows with coverings that could catch fire. Don't position the oven and microwave above shoulder height. They should have an adjacent heat-proof countertop where you can immediately set down anything hot. If you have small children, think twice before putting the cooktop on an island where hot burners and scalding food would be more accessible to them.

Be sure all cabinets are anchored firmly to wall studs. Plan for only lightweight items to be stored in cabinetry above your head and for safe storage of all dangerous implements and toxic chemicals.

Also consider how you'll store small appliances safely. One solution is to keep them out of reach in

appliance garages at countertop level. Plan safe knife storage too; never place knives in blocks that can be reached by small children.

Arrange for proper lighting. Adequate ambient lighting, along with task lighting, can minimize the kinds of accidents that may occur when you can't see well. Window shades or blinds can help control glare, and dimmer switches make it possible to set appropriate light levels.

Give careful consideration to the location and number of properly grounded outlets in order to eliminate the need for extension cords. Ideally, an outlet should be located every 4 feet along countertops but never next to the sink. All outlets must be protected by ground fault circuit interrupters (see page 191).

materials and appliances

Be aware that hard, angular, and slippery surfaces can be potentially hazardous. If small children or the elderly will be spending a good deal of time in the kitchen, plan on using materials that are forgiving in the event of a fall, such as resilient flooring, which softens impact and is relatively slip-resistant. To avoid bumps and bruises, particularly with small children, choose countertops with rolled edges and rounded corners, and flush cabinet pulls (or at least types without sharp edges). If you place an area rug in the kitchen, be sure it has a nonskid backing.

If you are buying a cooktop, consider one with burners that are staggered or in an L formation so you never have to reach across them. For the same reason, the controls should be positioned at the front or side. And, before you decide to buy a true "commercial" range, be aware that some types can get very hot to the touch.

To vent combustion gases from a gas stove, put in an adequately sized and powerful ventilation hood. Install a smoke detector between the kitchen and living areas, and mount a Class A-B-C fire extinguisher between the kitchen and an exit.

ABOVE: **Appliance garages conceal potentially dangerous small appliances; counters have rounded corners.**
LEFT: **Vinyl flooring is slip-resistant and resilient underfoot.**

Minimize the possibility of scalding by installing a faucet that is protected by an antiscald device or pressure-balancing valve. Or consider a new programmable faucet that allows you to set the water temperature you want. Choose a dishwasher that heats the water it uses for cleaning and rinsing; with one of these models, you can dial down your home's water heater to below 120 degrees, making baths and showers safer, too.

If you have small children, it's a good idea to factor in their inquisitiveness when you buy appliances. For example, if you plan to install a trash compactor, get the type that must be operated by a key and store the key out of their reach. Similarly, buy a dishwasher that is difficult for small children to open and operate. And locate the switch to the garbage disposal at the backsplash, where children can't reach it.

BELOW: **Childproof latches on lower doors make cabinets safer when small children are in the house.**

do-it-yourself guide

ONE OF THE EARLIEST DECISIONS YOU WILL MAKE IN YOUR REMODELING PLANNING
is how much of the work you'll do yourself. If you have basic skills and some experience,
there are plenty of good reasons to consider taking on some of the tasks. Your budget is
one. You will likely save some money, which can then be channeled into other aspects of
the process—a more expensive countertop or flooring material, for example. Also, you will
be able to exercise quality control over the job. A less tangible, but important, reward may
just be the enjoyment of doing the work itself, and the satisfaction of a job well done. You
may also learn something new in the process, or hone your skills.

While you are considering all the pluses, be aware of the realities. Do you have the skills
to do the tasks? A mistake, especially when it comes to walls and
wiring, may not only prove dangerous but can become more
costly to correct than if the work had been done by a profession-
al from the start. Do you have the right tools? If not, buying and renting what you will
need may end up costing you more in the long run. Are you able to complete the project in
a reasonable amount of time? Your free time is valuable, especially to your family, so be sure
to consider its worth as you make your decisions. You may simply decide to purchase the
materials yourself and take advantage of Lowe's professional installation services.

If you are able to answer "yes" to the questions above, taking on one or more of the
projects presented here may be the right choice for you. Four "families" of projects
are presented on the following pages: Wall and Ceiling Improvements, Plumbing
Updates, Electrical Updates, and Surface and Cabinet Improvements. They cover
basic tasks that most do-it-yourselfers should not find daunting. Each project is out-
lined with careful step-by-step illustrations or photographs to guide you along the
way. Be sure to take note of the warnings in the margins, and keep an eye out for
Lowe's Quick Tips, handy bits of advice designed to streamline your job.

Now, get to work!

tools and materials

BEFORE YOU LAUNCH INTO ANY DO-IT-yourself project, it's important to take stock of the tools and materials you'll need. Some modest improvements require only a few tools and materials, but extensive renovations will demand a selection that will allow you to handle nearly all aspects of construction, from tearing out old walls to hooking up electrical wiring and plumbing fixtures.

helpful tools

Shown here and on page 160 is a basic collection of key tools that can be used for a broad range of home improvements; you'll notice these tools are used repeatedly throughout this book's step-by-step projects. In the instructions for those projects, you'll find additional information about more-specialized tools you can rent or buy if you wish.

TAPE MEASURE

A 16- or 25-foot tape measure is sufficient for most jobs, but for laying out distances beyond 25 feet, choose a reel tape. The tape measure's end hook should be loosely riveted to adjust for precise "inside" and "outside" readings.

PLUMB BOB (TOP)

To use a plumb bob, hang it by a string from above and maneuver it close to the floor, without letting it touch the floor. Once the weight stops swinging, line up and mark the point. (It helps to have a partner at the other end.) This indicates perfect plumb.

COMBINATION SQUARE

A square helps you draw straight lines across lumber to be cut; it also helps you check angles on assembled pieces of a structure. A combination square is the most versatile type of square because it can check both 45- and 90-degree angles and serve as a ruler and a small level.

CAULKING GUN

For applying caulk and adhesives, use a caulking gun. For most jobs, a standard-sized one, which uses 10-ounce tubes, is the most convenient.

SCREWDRIVERS

The screwdriver vies with the hammer as the most frequently employed tool in a do-it-yourselfer's collection. It's important to have small, medium, and large tips in each main shape: standard, Phillips, and square drive (an ill-fitting tip may lead to a burred screw head or gouged work surface). If you'll be driving many screws, save your wrist by using a power drill with a screwdriver bit.

ADJUSTABLE WRENCH

You may be surprised at how often you'll reach for a wrench on a repair job—to drive lag screws, tighten bolts and nuts, or remove existing structures such as cabinets and built-ins. A 10- or 12-inch adjustable wrench is an excellent multi-purpose choice.

CROSSCUT SAW

A relatively short, multipurpose crosscut handsaw is convenient for small wood-cutting jobs. Look for a "taper ground" saw; the blade's thickness tapers toward the back and the tip, preventing the saw from binding in the kerf (saw cut) and allowing a narrower set to the teeth.

UTILITY KNIFE

A standard utility knife is helpful for many household repair and improvement jobs, including cutting drywall, vinyl flooring, and tile backerboard. Replace the blade frequently to ensure clean cuts.

CLAW HAMMER

Hammer faces may be either flat or slightly convex. The convex, or bell-faced, type allows you to drive a nail flush without marring the wood's surface. Mesh-type faces are available for rough framing work—the mesh pattern keeps the face from glancing off large nail heads and can help guide the nails, but don't use this face for finish work because the pattern will imprint the surface.

CHALK LINE

A chalk line is ideal for marking long cutting lines on sheet materials and laying out reference lines on a wall, ceiling, or floor. To mark a line, stretch the chalk-covered cord taut between two points. Then lift and snap it down sharply.

LEVEL

To test a horizontal surface for level, place a level on the surface; when the air bubble in the liquid enclosed in the center glass tubing lines up exactly between the two marks, consider the surface level. When the level is held vertically, the tubes near each end indicate plumb.

WORKING SAFELY

Here are a few important rules and practices to ensure the safe use of tools and materials:

SAFE WORKPLACE Work in a well-lit, uncluttered area. Keep tools and materials organized. Plan your setup carefully before you begin work. Whenever possible, avoid working with a partner in cramped quarters; you can too easily be injured by the swing of someone else's hammer. Clean up as you go.

TOXIC MATERIALS Some of the materials you encounter in improvements and repairs can be dangerous to your health: wood preservatives; oil-based enamel, varnish, and lacquer—and their solvents; adhesives (especially resorcinol, epoxy, and contact cement); insulation (asbestos fibers and urea formaldehyde); and even sawdust or the dust particles from wallboard joint compound. Read all the precautions on product labels, and follow them exactly. Ventilate the workplace adequately, and clean up the area frequently.

CLOTHING AND GEAR Wear sturdy clothing and the appropriate safety gear to avoid contact with dangerous materials (see more about safety gear on page 153). Always wear safety glasses when using power tools or tools that involve striking an object, such as when using a hammer and chisel.

POWER TOOL SAFETY Follow the manufacturer's specifications for using, cleaning, and lubricating power tools, and make sure all blades and bits are sharp and undamaged. Be absolutely certain to unplug any tool before servicing or adjusting it and after you've finished using it. Check that any safety devices, such as guards on the tool, are in good working order. To prevent shock, choose double-insulated tools (any power tool not double-insulated should be properly grounded). If you are working in a damp area or outdoors, a ground fault circuit interrupter (GFCI or GFI)—either the portable or built-in type—is essential.

EXTENSION CORDS Use the shortest extension cord you can for the job. A very long cord can overheat, creating a fire hazard. Furthermore, the longer the cord, the less amperage it will deliver, which translates into less power for the tool's motor. Be sure the extension cord is rated to handle the amperage load requirements of all the tools you plan to plug into it.

tools and materials

PORTABLE CIRCULAR SAW

Used for framing and many other construction jobs, this saw allows you to make straight cross-cuts much faster than with a handsaw and is unparalleled for ripping along the lengths of boards. The most common 7¼-inch model will go through surfaced 2-by framing lumber at any angle between 45 degrees and 90 degrees.

RECIPROCATING SAW

Ideal for roughing-in or demolition work, the reciprocating saw can be fitted with any of several blades to cut wood studs and joists, lath and plaster, steel pipe, and even nails. For precise control, choose a model with variable speeds.

POWER DRILL/DRIVER

An electric drill is classified by the biggest bit shank that can be accommodated in its chuck (jaws), most commonly ¼-inch, ⅜-inch, and ½-inch. For most jobs, a cordless ⅜-inch variable-speed drill is your best bet; it can handle a wide range of drill bits and accessories and makes an excellent power screwdriver when fitted with screwdriver bits.

SABER SAW

The saber saw's high-speed motor drives one of many types of blades in an up-and-down (recipro-cating) motion; the blade on an orbital model goes forward and up, then back on the down-stroke, for faster cuts. A saber saw excels at cutting curves, circles, and cutouts in a variety of materials but can also do straight cutting or beveling. Consider a variable-speed model for more control on tight curves and various materials.

materials

At Lowe's you'll discover an outstanding selection of lumber, fasteners, and other materials for your home improvement projects. In fact, the choices can be a bit overwhelming. So, to make your visit easier, we've provided here a basic primer on key materials:

LUMBER Lumber is divided into softwoods and hardwoods, terms that refer to the origin of the wood, not its hardness (though most hardwoods tend to be harder than softwoods). As a rule, softwoods are much less expensive, easier to tool, and more readily available than hardwoods, so softwoods are chosen for most construction. Hardwoods are used where beauty and hardness are important, such as for flooring, cabinets, and some trim.

At the mill, lumber is sorted and identified by name and, in many cases, the species and the grading agency. Generally, lumber grades are determined by a number of factors: natural growth characteristics or blemishes such as knots; defects caused by milling errors; and techniques used for drying and preserving wood that affect strength, durability, or appearance. The fewer the knots and other defects, the pricier a board. To save money on a project, pinpoint the lowest grade suitable for each component.

Lumber is normally stocked in lengths from 6 to 16 feet and in a broad range of widths and thicknesses. Note that the actual size of surfaced boards and dimension lumber is less than what is suggested by their names because of shrinkage during drying and surface planing. If you're unsure of actual sizes, either measure or check with a Lowe's salesperson.

NAILS Common nails, favored for construction, have an extra-thick shank and a broad head; finishing nails have a small head. Where you don't want a nail's head to show, choose a finishing nail (after you drive it nearly flush, sink the nail's head below the surface with a nail set). Choose hot-dipped galvanized nails where they may be exposed to moisture.

SCREWS Though they're more expensive than nails, screws offer several advantages for certain types of construction. They don't pop out as readily as nails, and their coating is less likely to be damaged during installation. With screws, you don't have to worry about hammer dents. Screws also are easier than nails to remove when repairs are required.

Usually black in color, drywall screws (also called multipurpose screws) come in many sizes and can be driven with an electric drill or screw gun with an adjustable clutch and Phillips-screwdriver tip. Galvanized deck screws are longer and have a coarser thread; they're suitable where exposed to moisture. These two types of screws are not rated for shear (or hanging) strength, so opt for nails, lag screws, or bolts for heavy construction.

Toggle bolts and hollow-wall fasteners that receive screws allow you to fasten securely to drywall and plaster. Toggle bolts, spreading anchors, and metal threaded anchors are the strongest.

The lag screw (also called a lag bolt) is a heavy-duty fastener with a square or hexagonal head; it is driven with a wrench or a ratchet and socket. Before driving a lag screw, predrill a lead hole about two-

HOLLOW-WALL FASTENERS

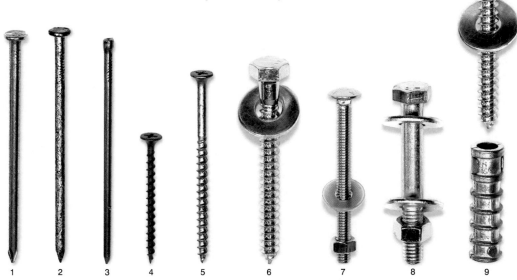

thirds the length of the screw, using a drill bit that's ⅛ inch smaller than the lag screw's shank. Slide a washer onto each lag screw before driving it.

BOLTS For heavy-duty fastening, choose bolts. Most are zinc-plated steel. Bolts go into predrilled holes and are secured by nuts. The machine bolt has a square or hexagonal head, a nut, and two washers; it must be tightened with a wrench at each end. The carriage bolt has a self-anchoring head that digs into the wood as the nut is tightened.

Expanding anchors allow you to secure wooden members to a masonry wall or slab floor. They feature expanding sleeves that grip the hole firmly when the bolt is driven home.

Bolts are classified by diameter (⅛ to 1 inch) and length (⅜ inch and up). To give the nut a firm bite, select a bolt ½ to 1 inch longer than the combined thickness of the pieces to be joined.

1. Toggle bolt
2. Spreading anchor
3. Threaded anchor (metal)
4. Threaded anchor (plastic)
5. Plastic sleeve
6. Winged sleeve

NAILS, SCREWS, AND BOLTS
1. Common nail
2. Galvanized nail
3. Finishing nail
4. Drywall screw
5. Deck screw
6. Lag screw and washer
7. Carriage bolt, washer, and nut
8. Machine bolt, washers, and nut
9. Lag screw, washer, and expanding lead anchor

wall and ceiling

A spectacular coffered
ceiling and upper walls,
produced from built-up
framing and molding,
give this kitchen a sense
of grandeur.

improvements

THERE ARE INSTANCES WHEN THE SUCCESSFUL KITCHEN makeover depends on the removal or addition of one or more walls. You may want to open up the kitchen to another room, for example, reposition or remove a doorway, or build a half wall to create a counter. Opening up a wall and building a new wall are accessible do-it-yourself projects, provided you understand a few basic principles of construction.

A home contains two types of walls. Some, aptly called bearing walls, are positioned and structured to help bear the weight of the house and the roof. Removal of these pivotal structures is the province of architects and professional builders only, since the weight borne by bearing walls must first be shifted and then supported elsewhere. Other walls, however, are nonbearing, meaning that they do not assist in holding the structure's weight. These can be removed, and built, more easily than you might imagine. Before removal of any wall, be sure to consult an architect, structural engineer, or qualified building contractor to determine whether the wall in question is bearing or nonbearing.

The projects on the following pages begin with step-by-step instructions on opening up an existing wall, including removing drywall, plaster, and non-load-bearing studs. Next are directions on building a simple wall, and hanging, finishing, and patching drywall, skills that apply to both wall and ceiling work. And finally, we tell you how to install interior trim, for that elegant finishing touch.

OPENING A WALL 164

BUILDING A WALL 166

HANGING DRYWALL 168

INSTALLING TRIM 172

These projects call for an assortment of carpentry tools, including a straight-claw framing hammer and a sharp wood chisel.

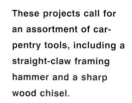

opening a wall

Removing a wall can make a dramatic difference in the openness of a kitchen. Here, a bearing wall was replaced by a beam.

FOR CERTAIN HOME IMPROVEMENTS, some demolition is necessary before you can begin new construction. So it is with walls, which occasionally need to be opened up, modified, or removed entirely. Doing this is relatively easy but guaranteed to make a mess. And, after you remove a wall, you will have to patch the floor, walls, and ceiling.

Before you remove any wall studs, you must determine whether or not the wall is a "bearing wall"—part of your home's structural system (see opposite).

If the wall is bearing, the opening it leaves must be engineered with the proper beams or headers to carry the loads no longer supported by the wall. For more about wall structure, see the illustration on page 167.

Be aware that obstructions within a wall may have impact on its removal. For example, if extensive plumbing resides where you are planning a doorway or pass-through, you might want to rethink the opening's location. Be ready for surprises; in many cases, you won't discover pipes or wires until you've removed the wall's surface material.

Before you begin, mask off the area with plastic sheeting to prevent the dust from permeating your home, and protect the floor with drop cloths. Turn off the electrical circuits that supply power to receptacles, light switches, or wires in the wall. Pry off any moldings. When the demolition begins, wear work gloves, protective goggles, and a dust mask.

Most walls are surfaced with gypsum wallboard (drywall). To remove it, punch through the center of the panel with a hammer and use a prybar to extract pieces. To dispose of plaster and lath, smash the plaster with a sledgehammer, then pry off the lath.

REMOVING A NONBEARING WALL

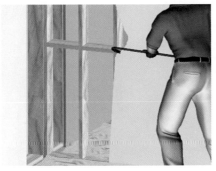

1 After prying the surface material off the wall studs, locate the studs on the adjoining wall that are on either side of the wall you're removing. Using a utility knife, slit through the taped drywall joints at the studs' centers. Remove the surface material between these studs. Pull any remaining nails from both walls' studs.

2 With the water and electrical circuits turned off, remove any wiring or plumbing from the wall and properly cap pipes and terminate circuits. If you're unfamiliar with this type of work, call an electrical or plumbing contractor. (See more about plumbing on pages 176–187 and wiring on pages 188–197.)

3 With a sledgehammer, knock out any fireblocks from between the studs, then sever the studs a few inches up from the floor with a reciprocating saw. Pull and twist the upper lengths of the studs to free them from the top plate. Using a hammer, knock over the short stud blocks at the base and pry them up. Pull out any protruding nails.

4 Cut through the end stud at a downward diagonal angle. Pry out the two pieces, beginning with the lower half, and pull them free from the top plate, the bottom plate, and the anchoring stud in the adjoining wall.

5 To remove the top plate, make a diagonal cut across it, then wedge the prybar between the two halves and pry them downward. If the top plate goes through the adjoining wall, first cut it flush with that wall's top plate. Pull out any nails.

6 Make an angled cut across the bottom plate, taking care not to cut the floor. As with the top plate, if the bottom plate goes through the adjoining wall, cut it flush at the end first. Pry up the plate and pull out any nails.

WHAT IS A BEARING WALL?

Walls are classified as either bearing or nonbearing. Bearing walls help carry the weight of the house, providing support to floors above. They should not be removed without a properly engineered method of support to replace them during and after removal—typically a system of beams. Nonbearing walls help shape the interior by defining rooms within the house and serving as conduits for essential plumbing and electrical systems. They may be removed without compromising the house's structure, though mechanical systems within the wall must be capped off or rerouted.

All exterior walls are bearing and many interior walls may also be bearing, especially in multilevel homes. Normally, at least one main interior wall, situated over a girder or interior foundation wall, is also bearing. If you are unsure whether or not an interior wall is a bearing wall or how to provide the necessary support when removing it, consult a local building professional before doing any demolition work.

building a wall

WHEN RECONFIGURING SPACE FOR A major kitchen-remodeling project, you may need to build one or more new interior walls. A simple wall can offer support to cabinets or just provide a sense of enclosure. The job is a relatively easy one, requiring basic carpentry skills and tools such as a hammer, combination square, and saw (ideally a power circular saw).

Depending on the nature of your floor, walls, and ceiling, you may have to peel away some surface materials to provide for secure attachment at the top, bottom, and one end of the new wall. If the new wall won't butt into studs at the connecting wall or fall directly beneath a ceiling joist, you must install nailing blocks between the framing to provide support for nailing.

A typical interior wall has a skeleton of vertical 2-by-4 studs that stand between a horizontal 2-by-4 base plate and a top plate, also a 2 by 4. The framework is covered with gypsum wallboard, lath and plaster, or other paneling materials.

first steps

Mark the centerline of the new wall across the ceiling. At each end of the line, make a mark 1¾ inches (half the width of the new wall's 2-by-4 top plate) in one direction, then snap a chalk line between the marks to create a guide for aligning the top plate.

Cut the bottom and top plates to length. Plan the locations of the studs (see step 1). Nail the plates in place (see steps 2 and 3). When nailing down the bottom

1 Lay the top and bottom plates side by side and mark perpendicular lines across them where each wall stud will go. Use a combination square so the studs will align perfectly. Plan one stud at each end and, beginning at the end that meets a wall, measure 15¼ inches to locate the inside edge of the first stud, then 16 inches to the same edge of each additional intermediate stud.

2 Hold the top plate in position along the chalk line marked on the ceiling and nail to each ceiling framing member with two 3½-inch nails. (Nail through the ceiling material and into joists or nailing blocks between joists.)

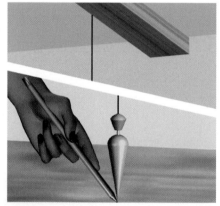

3 Establish the bottom plate's location directly beneath the top plate by hanging a plumb bob from each end of the ceiling's edge line to just above the floor, then marking the floor. Snap a chalk line along the floor between the marks to align the bottom plate's edge. Nail the bottom plate with 3-inch nails staggered and spaced every 16 inches.

plate, don't nail where a doorway will be. When attaching to a masonry floor, install masonry anchors every 2 or 3 feet.

Measure and cut the studs one at a time, making sure they fit precisely (see step 4). Measure, cut, and install fire blocks between the studs, 4 feet up from the floor on each wall stud, and stagger the blocks—one above, the next one below—the marks to make nailing easier.

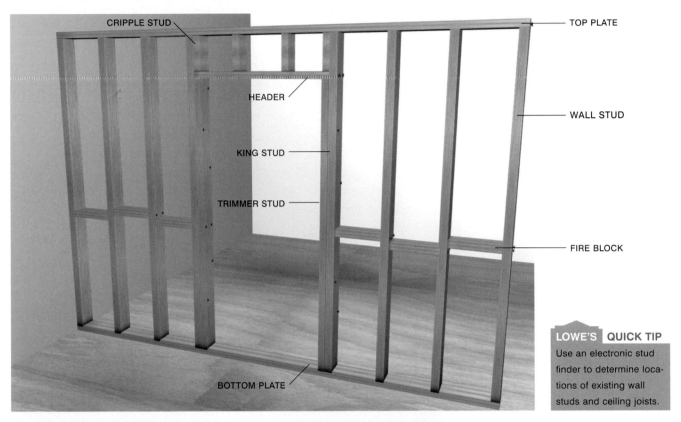

CRIPPLE STUD

TOP PLATE

HEADER

WALL STUD

KING STUD

TRIMMER STUD

FIRE BLOCK

BOTTOM PLATE

LOWE'S QUICK TIP
Use an electronic stud finder to determine locations of existing wall studs and ceiling joists.

4 To install each stud, lift into position, line up on its mark, check plumb using a carpenter's level, and nail into place. Use stud-framing clips, as shown, for easy fastening, or toenail each stud to both the top plate and the bottom plate with 2½-inch nails. Be sure to keep the edge of each stud flush with the faces of the top and bottom plates.

5 Where one wall intersects another, double-up studs, as shown above left, to receive the intersecting wall. If the wall will turn a corner, frame with two full-length studs and shorter blocks sandwiched between, as shown above right.

FRAMING A DOORWAY

- Measure half the width of the pre-hung door's rough opening in each direction from the doorway's centerline and mark for the inside edge of each trimmer stud. Measure 3½ inches farther to mark the inside edges of the king studs.
- Nail the full-length king studs to the plates on each side of the doorway.
- Cut the trimmer studs, then nail them to the king studs with 3-inch nails about every 12 inches in a staggered pattern.
- Nail the header to the trimmers and king studs and the cripples to the header and top plate.
- Use a handsaw to cut through the bottom plate, then remove the plate before installing the door's frame.

hanging drywall

BY FAR THE MOST COMMON FINISH material for walls and ceilings is drywall, also called gypsum board; a common trade name is Sheetrock®. Drywall comes in standard 4-by-8-foot sheets and in three thicknesses: $3/8$, $1/2$, and $5/8$ inch. The most common thickness for finishing a wall or ceiling is $1/2$ inch. For areas where moisture is a concern, such as kitchens and bathrooms, you can purchase water-resistant drywall that's identifiable by the green or blue paper covering its surface.

Cutting and installing drywall is fairly straightforward and can be accomplished with only a handful of common hand tools such as a utility knife, hammer or power drill driver, and putty knife. However, because full panels are heavy and awkward to work with, hanging dry-wall is far easier with a helper or two.

If you're covering both ceilings and walls, install the ceiling first—wall panels

CUTTING AND INSTALLING DRYWALL

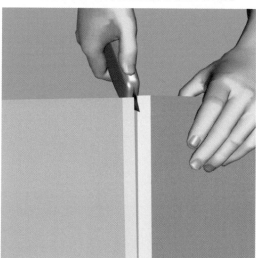

1 Using a pencil and straightedge or chalk line, mark your cutting line across the front paper layer. Score through the front paper with a utility knife, then turn the drywall over and break the gypsum core by bending toward the back. Finish by cutting the back paper along the crease, as shown.

2 When cutting drywall to fit around doorways, windows, outlets, and other surface interruptions, measure out from the adjacent panel and up from the floor to the obstruction, then transfer these measurements onto a new panel and cut. Make small cutouts for outlet and switch boxes about $3/16$ inch bigger than the boxes, and adjust the holes with a perforated rasp if necessary.

will help support the ceiling panels' edges. As shown here, you can use a utility knife to make straight cuts, and a compass saw, drywall saw, or power saber saw to make curved cuts or small cutouts.

You'll need to finish the joints and corners if the wall will be painted or wallpapered, but you may not need to hide joints on installations that serve as a backing for ceramic tile or cabinets.

fastening drywall

On ceilings, use annular ring nails or drywall screws to fasten drywall panels perpendicular to joists. On walls, use drywall nails or screws to attach panels horizontally to studs, top plate, and bottom plate. Panel joints should be centered over ceiling joists or wall studs and staggered so

that they don't align with adjacent joints. Before installing wall panels, mark wall-stud locations on the floor and ceiling so that you can find them easily after the panels are in place.

Driving screws with a screw gun or drill driver is easiest and fastest, particularly for ceilings. Most codes call for spacing fasteners every 8 inches along panel ends, edges, and intermediate supports. Position fasteners at least $\frac{3}{8}$ inch from panel edges.

If you nail the panels, use a bell-faced or drywall hammer to dimple the drywall surface with the final blow on each nail head (but don't puncture the paper on the surface). This creates a small divot that will be filled with drywall compound during finishing.

FASTENING DRYWALL

1 Position a pair of stepladders or set up sturdy sawhorses and planks to serve as a low scaffold. Then you and a helper can hold each end of a panel in place against the ceiling joists while you are fastening it. Start fastening near the center of each panel, then place a few fasteners at the edges to take the weight off, and continue until each panel is fully fastened.

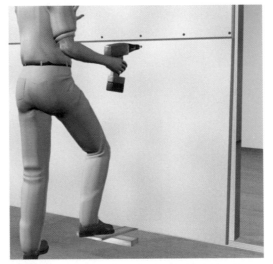

2 On walls, begin at one corner. Push the first panel tight against the ceiling, and nail or screw to the studs. Install the additional upper panels, then the lower ones. Force the lower panels tight against the upper ones when fastening them.

finishing drywall

The key challenge in finishing drywall is creating invisible seams where the edges of adjacent panels butt against each other. Although the techniques are simple to master, they require patience and attention to detail.

The joints between panels are covered with paper or self-adhesive mesh joint tape and thin coats of joint compound (commonly referred to as mud). Self-adhesive mesh tape can be applied directly over the joint; paper tape must be embedded in a thin coat of joint compound but costs less. Typically, you apply three layers of compound over the tape, each with a progressively wider-blade putty knife. Allow the compound to dry after each coat, then lightly sand.

When you're satisfied with the smoothness and flatness of the joints, let them dry completely, then seal the drywall with primer. Finally, apply the paint or wall covering of your choice.

On inside corners, apply a thin layer of compound to the drywall on each side of the corner and press precreased drywall tape into the corner with a corner tool or putty knife. Then treat as you would any other joint.

Cover outside corners with protective metal corner bead (made for drywall). Cut to length and nail through perforations every 12 inches. Feather out drywall compound (see step 2) along the metal edge in three coats as you would a regular joint but without applying drywall tape.

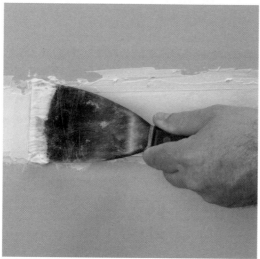

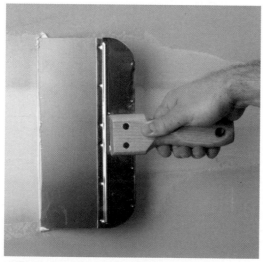

1 Press the paper tape into a thin coat of wet joint compound with a wide-blade putty knife, then apply a skim coat over the tape. Also, using a 2-inch putty knife, cover any nail or screw heads with joint compound.

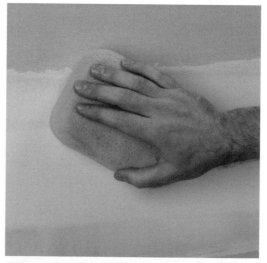

2 After the first coat has dried (typically overnight), sand lightly and apply two more coats, using a wider-blade knife with each succeeding coat. Work the compound gently away from the joint to feather it for a smooth transition.

3 Allow the joint compound to dry completely (again, typically overnight), then smooth the joints with medium, then fine, sandpaper or sanding screen. For a final smoothing, use a damp sponge, which doesn't generate dust so there's less mess.

LOWE'S QUICK TIP

Joint compound is much easier to work with if you use a "hawk"—a handled metal platform you load up with the compound and carry around as you go about your work.

patching drywall

The method you use to patch drywall will depend on the hole size. Small holes are easy to fix, as shown at right, but holes larger than an inch need a drywall patch. One of the simplest ways to patch larger holes is with a drywall repair kit that uses special clips to secure the patch to the wall, as shown in the three steps below.

1 Start by cutting out the damaged area with a drywall saw or by making a series of progressively deeper cuts with a utility knife.

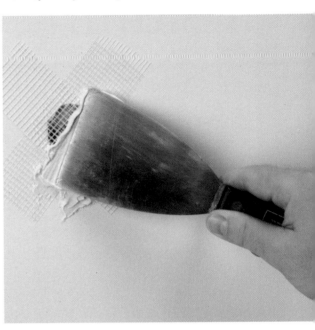

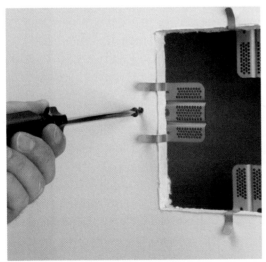

2 Slip the drywall repair clips onto the edges of the rectangular hole and screw into place. Be sure to drive the screw heads slightly below the surface of the drywall.

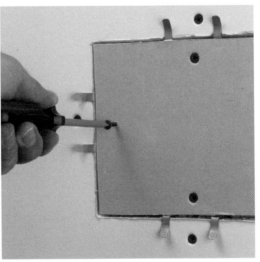

3 From a piece of drywall, cut a patch to fit the hole and attach to the drywall clips by driving screws through the patch into the clips. Finish the seams and cover the clips using the same methods as those for drywall joints (see opposite).

installing trim

Chair rail protects the wall from scrapes by chair backs and provides a measure of classic character.

CROWN MOLDING, CHAIR RAIL, AND similar molding and trim can add charm, style, and distinctive detailing to a kitchen. And, because trim is often installed where two surfaces or materials meet, it can produce attractive transitions while hiding joints or separations. Best of all, installing trim is relatively simple to do with a few basic tools.

The relative size and scale of the trim you choose should be in keeping with the size of the room—smaller for small rooms and larger for large spaces.

Regardless of the type of trim you install, you'll use the same methods for cutting, joining, attaching, and finishing the material. Whenever possible, prefinish trim before installation, then touch up afterward; this is infinitely easier than masking and painting trim in place.

cutting and joining trim

The simplest way to join two pieces at a corner is with a miter joint, where the ends are cut at a 45-degree angle, then butted together to make a 90-degree corner. You can cut a miter joint with an inexpensive miter box and handsaw, but the preferable tool is a power miter saw, shown opposite.

One problem with miter joints at corners is that, in order for the trim pieces to meet precisely, the room's walls must meet at a perfect right angle—which few do. You can try to measure the angle and adjust your cuts accordingly, but this can be both time-consuming and frustrating. A good alternative is a coped joint.

Taking its name from the tool used to make it—the coping saw—a coped joint creates a flawless joint at a corner regardless of the angle of the intersection. Of the two pieces that make up a coped corner joint, one is left square and butted into the corner; the other is "coped"—cut at a contour to match the profile of the molding, as shown below. If you're new to coping, practice on some scrap molding first. Cut the molding several inches longer than the finished length needed, to allow for a couple of tries.

In a perfect world, the coped piece will mate seamlessly with its companion piece. Chances are, though, that the coped end will need some fine-tuning. A rat-tail or round file, or a dowel wrapped with sandpaper works well for making minor adjustments. Check the fit frequently to make sure you don't remove too much wood.

To join two pieces together end-to-end on a long wall, use a scarf joint, as shown at right. The beauty of the scarf joint is that it marries the ends of the two pieces with an almost invisible seam.

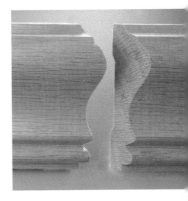

MAKING A SCARF JOINT

To make a scarf joint, simply miter-cut the ends of the pieces to be joined at opposing angles. Then slide the two pieces together and fasten them with glue and finish nails.

COPING A JOINT

1 To cope a joint, start by placing the molding upside down on the miter saw and cutting the end at a 45-degree angle. This will reveal the profile that you need to cope.

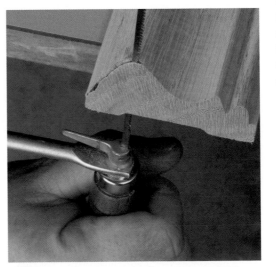

2 Now comes the tricky part. Hold the coping saw so it's at a 90-degree angle to the molding and begin cutting the end. The idea is to follow the contour of the cut edge with the saw blade.

installing trim

nailing trim

Trim is attached to walls and ceiling with finish nails. Professional trim carpenters use air nailers, which drive and set a nail with a pull of the trigger. In addition, an air nailer fitted with a no-mar tip will never ding or dent the molding the way a hammer can.

If you're planning to install a lot of trim, you might consider renting or buying an air nailer. If you're installing a modest amount of trim, however, a hammer and a nail set will work just fine.

After the trim is in place, fill the nail holes with wood putty and touch up with paint if needed.

caulking trim

No matter how precisely you install trim, you'll probably find places where gaps show up between the trim and the wall or ceiling. Due to surface variations, these are to be expected. Seal the gaps with caulk, as shown at bottom.

ATTACHING TRIM

1 Because wood trim is often quite thin, it is prone to splitting when a nail is driven through it. To prevent this, drill a pilot hole slightly smaller than the nail's diameter. Then, drive the nail in with a hammer, stopping when the head is about ½ inch from the molding's surface.

2 Finish driving the nail below the surface with a nail set and hammer, as shown, so you won't mar the trim. When all of the trim is in place, fill in all the nail holes with wood putty and touch up with paint or other finish if necessary.

CAULKING GAPS
If you intend to paint after installing molding, run a bead of latex caulk between trim and the wall or ceiling, not only for appearances but also to seal up any drafts that might be caused by air moving through the wall. Smooth with your finger and wipe off any excess.

installing chair rail

Chair rail was originally designed to prevent chair backs from marring walls; nowadays it's largely used as a decorative accent. Even if you're installing it only for looks, it should be mounted the correct distance from the floor—traditionally, between 32 and 36 inches. For chair rail that will be used to protect walls, determine the best height by placing one of your chairs against the wall and making a mark at the point of contact.

Begin the installation by drawing a level line around the perimeter of the room, then locating and marking studs, as shown at right.

Cut the chair rail to length. Cope the joints at the corners and scarf together pieces where they meet along a wall. Drill pilot holes through the rail and into the wall studs, then secure each piece with 2-inch finish nails. For added stability, apply a thin bead of construction adhesive to the back of the railing before nailing.

installing crown molding

Traditionally reserved for public rooms, crown molding is becoming increasingly popular in the kitchen, not only between walls and ceiling but also as a decorative accent at the tops of cabinets. As a general rule, choose crown molding that is 3 to 4 inches wide for a standard 8-foot ceiling, wider if your ceiling is vaulted.

Crown molding is cut and coped much like chair rail or baseboard. But because the molding has only two flat surfaces on the back side, it's tricky to hold while cutting. The best way to make accurate cuts is to build a cradle for the miter saw. This is nothing more than a couple of plywood scraps screwed together with a cleat attached to the base to hold the molding at the proper angle. When cutting the molding to expose a profile for coping, insert the molding in the cradle upside down and backward.

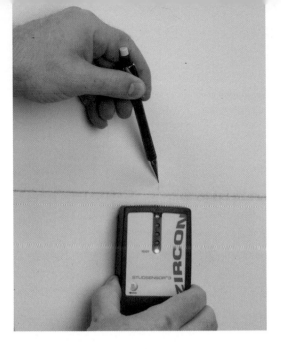

PREPARING TO INSTALL CHAIR RAIL
Draw a line around the perimeter of the room, checking for level, then locate the wall studs and mark their locations.

LOWE'S QUICK TIP
Gaps at mitered joints can be closed by "burnishing" the joint with the shank of a screwdriver—press firmly to crush the wood fibers so they fill in the gap.

INSTALLING CROWN MOLDING

1 Locate the positions of the wall studs and the ceiling joists, press the flats of the molding against wall and ceiling, drill pilot holes, then drive in finishing nails. Use a nail set to recess nail heads.

2 If your ceiling joists run parallel to the wall, you'll have to use one of two alternate methods to secure the top of the molding. The first is to apply a bead of construction adhesive to the top flat.

3 For a more secure hold, cut scraps of wood blocking to fit behind the molding and attach these to the wall studs with 3-inch drywall screws. Then attach the molding to the blocking with finish nails.

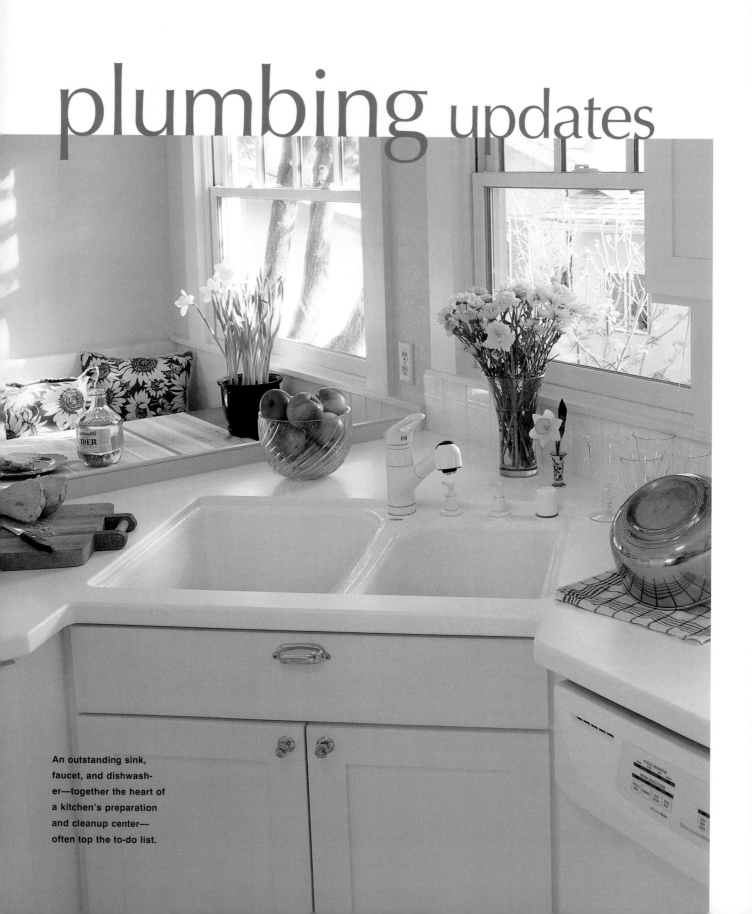

plumbing updates

An outstanding sink, faucet, and dishwasher—together the heart of a kitchen's preparation and cleanup center— often top the to-do list.

WHILE INSTALLING A PLUMBING SYSTEM FROM SCRATCH IS best left to professionals—in fact, some jurisdictions insist that plumbing contractors do the work and permits are required—there are some projects that do-it-yourselfers can readily complete. Indeed, all homeowners would do well to know how to install a basic faucet set, since it's likely easier to do it yourself than to find a plumber willing to come out for such a small job.

Short of running pipes under floorboards, common plumbing tasks fall into two categories: installation and hookups. The projects presented on the following pages include how to install a drop-in stainless-steel sink, a faucet, and a garbage disposal. They involve the simplest pipe-fitting skills and require only a few tools. Also included are step-by-step instructions for hooking up a dishwasher and a water-treatment device.

Note that the garbage disposal and dishwasher installations require electrical connections. If you are not comfortable working with electricity, you may want to hook up the plumbing yourself and then either consult with or hire a professional electrician to complete the job.

The rule of thumb for working with plumbing is to make sure the water is shut off at its source before you begin. If you are working around electrical wires, especially when replacing an existing dishwasher or garbage disposal, be sure to turn off the electrical circuit for that area before you start, since water and electricity can be a lethal combination.

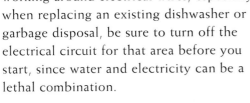

An adjustable wrench and screwdriver are two of the few tools needed for these projects.

installing a sink

TO MANY HOMEOWNERS, INSTALLING a sink seems like a daunting task, but the fact is, if you can trace around a template and cut out a hole, you can install a kitchen sink. You do want to make sure your new sink fits your countertop and the cabinet below it, so measure the width and depth of your lower cabinets before

making a purchase. Generally, a sink up to 22 inches deep (from front to back) will fit in a standard 24-inch-deep cabinet if you have no backsplash; if you do have a backsplash, your countertop will only take a sink up to 20½ inches deep. Of course, your options will increase if you are also changing your cabinetry and countertop.

Installing an easy-to-maintain stainless-steel sink in a laminate countertop is a relatively easy job.

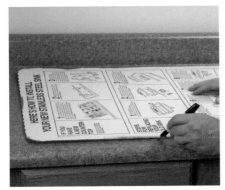

1 The first step when installing a new sink is to properly site the opening. Most sink manufacturers provide a template. Position the template so it is centered on the sink cabinet and is at least 1½ inches back from the countertop's front edge. If your countertop is deeper than 24 inches, place it farther back, but not more than 4 inches. Tape the template in place, then outline it with a marker.

2 After marking the opening, remove the template and drill a ⅜-inch-diameter hole in each corner. Insert a saber-saw blade in one of the holes and start cutting along the inside of the line. To prevent the cutout from snapping off and falling through as you complete the cuts, first screw a scrap of wood from front to back on the top of the cutout long enough so it spans the opening, plus a couple of inches. When you've finished, simply lift the cutout from the template.

3 Install the faucet (see pages 180–181 for instructions) and the sink strainers. (Doing this when you've got full access to the sink will be much easier than fitting the pieces in from below after the sink is installed.) Next, to create a watertight seal between the sink and the countertop, apply a bead of silicone caulk or plumber's putty around the entire perimeter of the underside of the sink's lip.

4 Carefully flip the sink over and insert into the opening, taking care not to disturb the caulk or putty. If your sink is heavy, get help lifting and installing it; also consider placing a couple of scraps of wood near the edge of the opening to support the sink and protect your fingers as you drop it into position.

5 Most sinks are pulled down tight against the countertop with special mounting clips that hook onto the lip on the underside of the sink and are tightened with a screwdriver or nutdriver. Follow the manufacturer's directions for spacing these clips. Tightening the mounting clips may cause the caulk or putty to squeeze out from under the sink lip, so remove this excess with a clean, soft rag.

6 To complete the project, first connect the P-trap. Join the faucet lines to the hot and cold supply lines with flexible supply tubes and connect the strainers to the waste line. Turn the water on at the shut-off valves, remove the aerator from the faucet, then turn on the water from the faucet to flush the system. Reinstall the aerator after you've run the water for a minute or so.

mounting a faucet

This single-handle sink faucet features a spout that pulls out to become a sprayer.

THE MAIN DETERMINANT OF HOW EASY or difficult it is to install a kitchen faucet is access. Installing a faucet into a new sink is simple because you can do it before setting the sink in place, with full access to the faucet parts, including the hard-to-reach mounting nuts. If the sink is already in place, replacing a faucet can be a challenge since your only access is from under the sink. This will require you to lie on your back and work around the supply lines to get to the mounting nuts that will secure the faucet. Even with the aid of a nifty tool called a basin wrench that extends your reach, it's still an awkward task. Depending on your circumstance, you may find it easier in the long run to remove the sink first.

After installing your new faucet, remove the aerator from the faucet and flush the lines to ensure that any debris does not clog and reduce the water flow. On a standard faucet, simply unscrew the aerator at the end of the spigot and let the water run for a minute or two. With a pullout sprayer faucet, the aerator/filter is housed in an inlet in the sprayer head. Just unthread the hose, remove the aerator/filter, and flush.

LOWE'S QUICK TIP
Flexible supply tubes make connecting a faucet a snap—with these, you don't have to do any cutting or fitting.

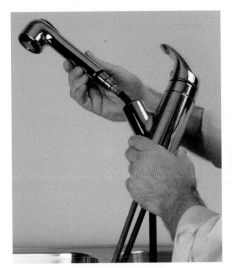

1 Many new faucets require some assembly before mounting to the sink; if that is the case, follow the manufacturer's directions. With most pullout sprayer faucets, the sprayer needs to be threaded through the faucet body first.

2 Insert the rubber gasket between the base plate of the faucet and the sink top to create a watertight seal. If no gasket is provided, pack the cavity of the faucet with plumber's putty, then insert the faucet body through the holes in the sink top. Thread the mounting nuts provided onto the faucet shafts, then center the threaded shafts in the sink's holes and tighten the nuts firmly.

3 Many manufacturers include a special long socket specifically to aid in tightening the mounting nuts. A hole in the socket accepts the shank of a screwdriver, guiding it as you tighten the nuts. If you're mounting the faucet on an installed sink, use this method.

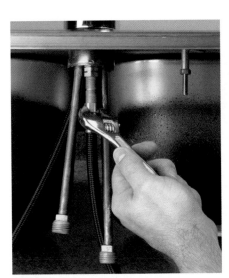

4 If you're installing a pullout sprayer faucet—or a faucet with a separate sprayer—now is the time to connect the sprayer to the faucet body. Check the manufacturer's directions to see if using pipe-wrap tape for this connection is recommended. Use an adjustable wrench to tighten the connection.

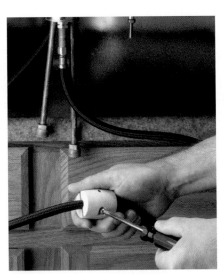

5 Most pullout sprayer faucets and faucets with separate sprayers come with a counterweight that attaches to the sprayer hose. This weight helps retract the hose back in to the sink cabinet after you've used the sprayer. Follow the manufacturer's directions on where to secure the weight, and take care not to crimp the hose as you attach the weight.

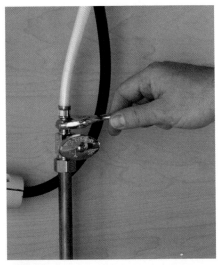

6 Hook up the faucet's hot and cold supply lines to the water supply shut-off valves under the sink. If necessary, gently bend the copper tubes coming out of the faucet for better access and connect flexible supply tubes to them. Simply wrap a couple of turns of pipe-wrap tape around the threaded nipples on the valves and connect the tubes. Tighten the nuts with an adjustable wrench.

installing a dishwasher

FOR A MODESTLY EXPERIENCED DO-IT-yourselfer, installing a built-in dishwasher is a pretty simple job requiring only a few hand tools and a spare afternoon.

Be sure your dishwasher's location will allow its door to swing open without hitting an adjacent cabinet or cabinet pulls.

Dishwashers come with the manufacturer's installation instructions; follow these exactly. The directions given here are meant to be a general guide.

electrical requirements

A 120-volt electrical receptacle or electrical box that is GFCI (ground fault circuit interrupter) protected must be located nearby, usually at the back of the sink base cabinet. If needed, have an electri-cian install or verify a grounded 15-amp receptacle, or you can wire your own according to the instructions on page 191.

plumbing hookups

The dishwasher must connect to the sink's hot-water supply, usually via a ⅜-inch-outside-diameter copper tube. A flexible drain hose runs from the dishwasher's waste outlet to a tee above the sink's drain trap or to a dishwasher inlet on a garbage disposal (sealed with a "knockout" plug that's removed for a dishwasher hookup). If your disposal has never been connected to a dishwasher, unplug it or turn off its circuit and use an old screwdriver to punch out the knockout plug, located inside the dishwasher nipple.

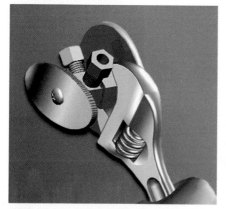

1 To install a shutoff valve for the dishwasher, first shut off the house's main valve. Disconnect the sink water supply tube from the valve, drain it into a bucket, then unscrew the shutoff valve from the supply nipple with a wrench. Wind pipe-wrap tape around the nipple's threads and screw a new dual-outlet valve onto it.

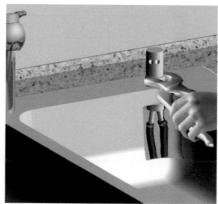

2 Install the air gap through a properly sized unused hole in the sink top (punch out the hole plug with a hammer). Insert the air gap, then using slip-joint pliers secure it from above with a locknut and push its cover into place.

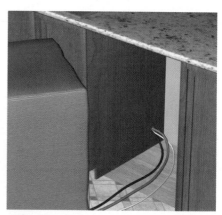

3 Position the dishwasher near its opening, and then push the hose, supply tube, and power cord through holes drilled in the back corner of the sink base cabinet. As you walk the dishwasher into place, be careful not to pinch or tangle these connectors.

The dishwasher can drain directly into the sink's trap if you don't have a disposal. Replace a section of the sink drain's tailpiece with a dishwasher tailpiece, which has a short T-shape nipple that connects to the dishwasher's drain hose. Cut the bottom of the sink's tailpiece with a hacksaw or tubing cutter and connect the new tailpiece with slip nuts and washers.

air gap

To prevent wastewater from draining or siphoning back into the dishwasher, many local codes require that it be connected to an air-gap fixture before the disposal. The air gap, bought separately, mounts on top of the sink or counter right next to the sink and connects to two flexible hoses— one that runs to the dishwasher's drain, the other to the sink's trap or the dishwasher inlet on the disposal. In some areas, codes allow looping the dishwasher's drain hose in a high arc up under the countertop as an alternative to installing an air gap.

If your sink doesn't have an unused hole for mounting the air gap, you'll need to bore one in the countertop next to the sink, using an electric drill and a hole saw, or have the sink top professionally drilled.

installation

If you are replacing a dishwasher, remove the old one first, reversing the installation instructions discussed here. Before doing any work, first unplug the appliance or turn off the circuit breaker and disconnect the power. Then turn off the water supply valve (usually located under the sink) or turn off the main house shutoff and drain the supply pipes by opening the faucet.

If there isn't a dedicated shutoff valve for the dishwasher, replace the existing shutoff valve with a special dual-outlet shutoff like the one shown in step 1.

Drill holes at the back lower corner of the sink base cabinet for the drain hose, water supply tube, and power cord.

After installation, adjust the dishwasher's front feet to level the appliance and align it with the cabinets and countertop. Anchor the unit to the underside of the counter with the screws provided. Restore water pressure and check for leaks. Install the dishwasher's front panel. Plug in (or hardwire) the unit.

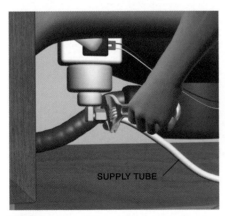

4 Reconnect the sink's supply tube to the dual-outlet valve, and connect the flexible supply tube to the valve's second outlet and the dishwasher's inlet. Then tighten with an adjustable wrench until snug.

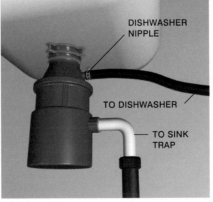

DISHWASHER NIPPLE

TO DISHWASHER

TO SINK TRAP

5 Slip one hose clamp over each end of the short drain hose that will run from the disposal to the large outlet on the air gap and cinch the clamps until tight. Then do the same with the longer drain hose, running it from the smaller outlet on the air gap to the drain fitting at the base of the dishwasher.

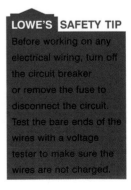

installing a disposal

ALTHOUGH NOT THE MOST GLAMOROUS kitchen improvement, the addition of a garbage disposal will be greatly appreciated by the chef of the house.

Because disposals vary greatly in size and bowl depth, check the dimensions to make sure the disposal you've chosen will fit under your sink.

Since installing a disposal requires both plumbing and electrical skills, it's a project best taken on by experienced do-it-yourselfers. One way to simplify the task is to have a licensed electrician install a GFCI (ground fault circuit interruptor; see page 191) outlet under the sink and a separate wall switch adjacent to the sink—then the only electrical work left is to wire a power cord to the disposal.

Always shut off the power to the circuit that will serve the disposal before beginning any work. If you're replacing a disposal, turn off the electricity to that circuit and unplug the disposal or disconnect the wiring before removing the unit.

LOWE'S | QUICK TIP
When working under a sink, temporarily remove the cabinet doors and set them aside to provide better access.

SNAP RING

1 First, disconnect and remove the existing waste assembly, from the sink flange to the trap. Have towels and a bucket handy to catch water and debris. Once the waste lines are out of the way, remove the mounting assembly from the disposal and install the new flange in the sinkhole, applying a coil of plumber's putty around it before dropping it into place, as shown.

2 Attach the upper mounting assembly to the sink flange, placing a heavy object such as a large phone book on top of the flange to hold it in place. Follow the manufacturer's directions for gasket placement and slip the mounting ring over the flange. Then, slide the snap ring onto the flange until it pops into the groove on the flange. Next, tighten the three mounting screws, as shown, until the assembly has a tight seal against the sink.

DISHWASHER NIPPLE

DISCHARGE TUBE

3 To get ready to attach the disposal to the mounting assembly, first attach the discharge tube, as shown. Then, inspect the P-trap and clean out any hardened waste. Next, prepare the dishwasher drain connection. This usually entails knocking out a drain plug from the dishwasher nipple and attaching the drain hose from the dishwasher.

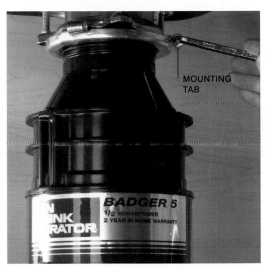

MOUNTING TAB

BADGER 5
1/2 HORSEPOWER
2 YEAR IN-HOME WARRANTY

IN SINK ERATOR

4 Position the disposal under the mounting assembly so that the mounting tabs can slide over the mounting tracks. Lift the disposal and insert the top into the mounting assembly. Rotate the lower mounting ring until all three mounting tabs lock over ridges in the mounting ring. Use the wrench provided or a screwdriver to tighten the ring.

TRAP

5 Rotate the disposal so that the discharge tube aligns with the drain trap. If your sink is a double-bowl model, you'll need to replumb the wasteline to attach to the disposal. If you're lucky, all you'll need is an extension tube. If not, you may need to replace the entire assembly, shown here.

6 Finally, connect the disposal to power. Either run a line or have a licensed electrician run power into the sink cabinet and install a GFCI receptacle (for more on this, see page 191). If your disposal didn't come with a plug on the end of the cord, wire the recommended grounded electrical cord to the disposal. Plug into the receptacle.

LOWE'S SAFETY TIP
Before working on the receptacle or wires connected to it, turn off the circuit breaker or remove the fuse to disconnect the circuit. Test the bare ends of the wires with a voltage tester to make sure they are not charged.

adding a water filter

INSTALLING A WATER-TREATMENT DEVICE is becoming one of the more popular kitchen upgrades. Many types of treatment devices are currently available, ranging from simple in-line cartridges to reverse-osmosis systems with undersink storage tanks. In between these are easy-to-install dual-cartridge devices. This type of system requires no electrical power, hooks up directly to your cold-water line, and installs in a few hours. Keep in mind,

however, that cartridge-based devices require you to periodically change the cartridges. If you notice changes in taste, odor, and/or water flow, that's a sure sign the cartridges need replacing.

A reverse-osmosis unit is hooked up similarly to the dual-cartridge device shown here, but it must also be connected to the sink's drain because it discharges wastewater. It stores clean water in a tank beneath the sink.

1 Start by mounting the dispenser. Most are designed to fit in the extra hole in a sink top, as shown, but if this hole is already occupied, you'll have to drill another in the sink or countertop. Follow the manufacturer's directions for the location and size of the hole. Drill only into stainless-steel or porcelain cast-iron sinks; if you have an all-porcelain sink, drill for the dispenser through the countertop.

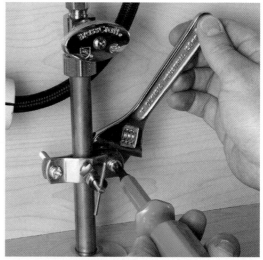

2 Tap into the existing cold-water supply line via a saddle valve, as shown. To install a saddle valve, first turn off the water supply, then open the faucet to drain the line. Following the manufacturer's directions, drill a small hole in the supply line. Turn the handle on the valve to expose the lance that's designed to puncture the pipe, and position the valve over the pipe so that the lance fits in the hole. Attach the back plate of the valve and tighten the nuts to lock in place, then screw in the lance.

3 Position the cartridge filtration unit roughly between the cold-water line and the dispenser. Be sure to leave the specified clearance between the system and the cabinet bottom to allow for cartridge replacement. Secure the device to the cabinet back or wall with the screws provided.

4 To hook up the device, start by cutting a length of plastic tubing to reach between the saddle valve and the system. Make it short enough not to kink, but long enough to allow for installing a new compression fitting (the connector shown at the end of the tubing) later if needed. Press the tubing into the compression fitting and thread onto the saddle valve; tighten with an adjustable wrench.

5 Insert the opposite end of the tubing into another compression fitting and thread onto the inlet port of the filtration unit. Tighten the nut with your hand, then make another turn or turn and a half with an adjustable wrench.

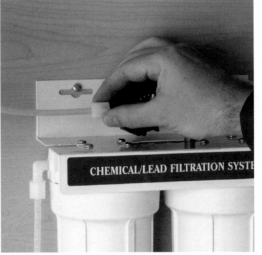

6 Finally, cut a piece of tubing to run from the outlet port of the system to the water dispenser. Insert compression fittings on both ends and thread the nuts onto the dispenser and the system. Turn on the water supply and open the water dispenser. Let the water run for about five minutes to flush out any carbon particles or air pockets. Most manufacturers recommend allowing the water to run for about 20 seconds before using.

LOWE'S QUICK TIP

When shopping for a water-treatment device, look for one with a built-in indicator that tells you when it's time to replace the filter cartridges.

electrical and

A striking combination
of standard- and low-
voltage lighting paints
this kitchen with a
dramatic palette of light.

lighting updates

TODAY'S KITCHEN, WITH ITS MULTIPLE USES AND MULTITUDE of appliances and media outlets, is usually the most intense electricity consumer of any room in the house. Remodeling, particularly of homes 30 years and older, invariably involves electrical work of some sort. Older kitchens may work off two ungrounded circuits, while newer kitchens can demand six or seven circuits, all of which need to be grounded to avoid electric shock hazards.

Very involved rewiring projects require permits and should be handled by professionals or very well trained amateurs. However, much of the basic electrical work can adequately and safely be handled by the do-it-yourselfer. The projects presented on the following pages—wiring receptacles, wiring switches, replacing a light fixture, and mounting an undercabinet light—all fall into that category.

The tools needed for basic electrical work are few and relatively inexpensive. If you are thinking about purchasing new tools, for added personal protection consider specialized insulated hand tools, colored bright orange and marked "1000" for their ability to withstand current to 1,000 volts.

Before you begin, be sure to study the step-by-step instructions carefully, and watch for the red cautionary notes in the margins. Electrical systems tend to be standardized, so there should be few surprises. If you do come across wiring that is a jumbled mess, call in a professional, since it likely was jury-rigged under a previous ownership, probably isn't to code, and may even be dangerous.

WIRING RECEPTACLES 190

WIRING SWITCHES 192

REPLACING A LIGHT 194

ADDING TASK LIGHTING 196

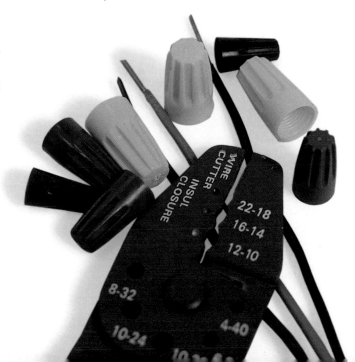

Electrical updates often require little more than new connections. You'll need wire strippers and wire nuts like these.

wiring receptacles

BECAUSE NEW KITCHENS ARE LOADED with electrical devices, a common task when remodeling a kitchen is wiring new or replacement receptacles. Receptacles are rated for voltage and amperage—usually 120 volts, and either 15 or 20 amps. Therefore, when you're replacing a receptacle, make sure to look at the back of the existing one to find the voltage and amperage ratings so that you can install an identical part.

Take note that in most municipalities, code requires that all kitchen countertop receptacles be GFCIs (ground fault circuit interrupters; see sidebar opposite). Code also requires that new receptacles be properly grounded. Don't replace an old-style two-prong outlet with a new, grounded three-prong outlet without first having an electrician run a ground wire to the electrical box. Without it, the circuit will be unsafe.

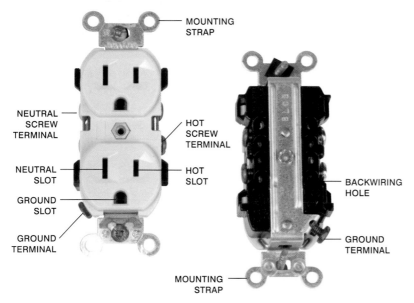

MOUNTING STRAP

NEUTRAL SCREW TERMINAL

HOT SCREW TERMINAL

NEUTRAL SLOT

HOT SLOT

GROUND SLOT

BACKWIRING HOLE

GROUND TERMINAL

GROUND TERMINAL

MOUNTING STRAP

RECEPTACLE HOOKUP

Receptacles have three colored screw terminals: brass, silver, and green. The brass terminals are for the hot wires, the silver are for neutral wires, and the green are for ground. Newer receptacles offer two ways to secure the wires: 1) wrap the stripped wire around the terminal before tightening it against the receptacle body, or 2) use the push-in terminals at the back of the receptacle.

END-OF-RUN RECEPTACLE

Installing or replacing a receptacle at the end of a run is a simple wiring task because only one set of wires needs to be connected. The black wire (hot) is attached to the brass terminal and the white wire (neutral) is attached to the silver terminal. The ground wire (usually bare) is attached to the green grounding lug.

MIDDLE-OF-RUN RECEPTACLE

A receptacle in the middle of a run will have two sets of wires to connect: One set brings in power, the other sends it along to the next receptacle. There are two ways to wire a mid-run receptacle. One method is to connect one set of wires to each pair of terminals, then pigtail the ground wires together and attach them to the grounding lug. The other method is to connect short jumper wires to the incoming and outgoing wires with wire nuts, then connect just the jumper wires to the terminals of the receptacle. This method makes it easier to replace the receptacle but requires a box deep enough to hold both sets of wires, the jumper wires, and wire nuts.

FINISHING THE INSTALLATION

After you've made the electrical connections, you are ready to attach the receptacle to the box and add the cover plate. Take care when you press the wires into the box to not inadvertently crimp a wire, which will create a short, or open, circuit. When you affix the cover plate, tighten the mounting screws just enough to hold it in place; if you overtighten a screw, you may crack the plate.

BUILT-IN PROTECTION: GFCI

A ground fault circuit interrupter is an electronic device that monitors a circuit for ground faults and shuts it down when one is detected. A ground fault is what happens when the current flowing into a circuit and the current flowing out of the circuit are not the same; in other words, some current is flowing outside the circuit, creating a hazard to property or to persons. GFCIs protect the devices plugged into them as well as those "forward" on the circuit.

Wiring a GFCI is similar to wiring a standard receptacle except the terminals are labeled "line" and "load." To protect a single location, attach the incoming pair of black and white wires to the "hot" and "white" (neutral) terminals on the "line" end. For protecting several outlets, the incoming wires are connected the same way, but the outgoing pair of black and white wires attach to the "load" end.

Multiple-outlet protection is susceptible to erroneous tripping when normal electrical fluctuations occur—which can be annoying because you have to reset the circuit every time.

wiring switches

WHEN UPDATING A KITCHEN'S LIGHTING scheme, you'll probably need to install or replace light switches—or update them with dimmer switches. The two most common types of switches used throughout the home are single-pole and three-way. A single-pole switch controls one or more lights from one location; three-way switches control lights from two locations.

As with receptacles, switches are rated for a specific voltage and amperage.

Whenever you replace a switch, look on the back for these ratings and purchase one that matches them.

Unlike receptacles, switches are wired only with hot (charged) wires, which means they open and close the hot leg (normally the black wire) of a circuit to allow current flow to the light. Sometimes a white wire is used to make this connection, but it should be painted black or wrapped with black electrical tape.

SINGLE-POLE SWITCH

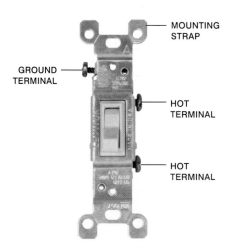

- MOUNTING STRAP
- GROUND TERMINAL
- HOT TERMINAL
- HOT TERMINAL

THREE-WAY SWITCH

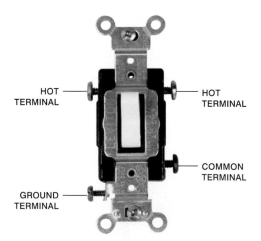

- HOT TERMINAL
- HOT TERMINAL
- GROUND TERMINAL
- COMMON TERMINAL

SINGLE-POLE AND THREE-WAY SWITCHES

To tell the difference between a single-pole and a three-way switch, simply count the number of terminals. A single-pole switch will have two (and a ground terminal), while a three-way will have three (and a ground terminal). Most newer switches allow for connections via push-in terminals at the back of the switch.

SINGLE-POLE-SWITCH WIRING

Wiring a single-pole switch could not be easier. Both terminals are brass, and the hot wires can be connected to either one. Occasionally, the wires running into the electrical switch box will be black (or red) and white. In such cases, wrap a piece of black electrical tape around the white wire (or paint it black) to indicate that it's hot.

THREE-WAY-SWITCH WIRING

A three-way switch has two brass terminals and one darker terminal labeled "common." To wire a three-way switch, connect the hot wire from the service panel or subpanel to the darker terminal. Then connect the hot wire from the lighting fixture to the darker terminal of the other switch. Wire the remaining terminals by running hot wires from the brass terminals on one switch to the brass terminals on the other switch.

MOUNTING A SWITCH OR DIMMER

To mount a switch or dimmer in the electrical box, make sure the switch is oriented correctly, then gently press the wires in (a three-way switch is unmarked so it can be mounted either side up). After the switch is in place, add the cover plate, taking care not to overtighten the screws, as that can crack the plate.

WIRING A DIMMER

Dimmer switches can be wired into existing circuits in the same way as the switches they replace. There are both single-pole and three-way dimmers. When selecting one, make sure it's designed for the type of lighting you want to control—dimmers are different for incandescent, fluorescent, and halogen lights. Wiring a dimmer is easy because most come with short jumper wires that connect to the existing wiring via wire nuts.

LOWE'S SAFETY TIP

Before working on any electrical wiring, turn off the circuit breaker or remove the fuse to disconnect the circuit. Test the bare ends of the wires with a voltage tester to make sure the wires are not charged.

replacing a light

ONE OF THE SIMPLEST—AND MOST overlooked—kitchen improvements is replacing the overhead lighting. Older fixtures not only give a kitchen an outdated look, they usually do a poor job of lighting the space.

Even if you've never worked with electricity before, you can replace a ceiling light fixture with ease. Indeed, the hardest part is selecting a new fixture from the myriad choices. To help narrow the selection, look for a fixture that will blend in well with your home's decor and provide the most useful light.

Before you begin, find the circuit breaker or fuse that powers the light. Turn off the circuit breaker or remove the fuse to shut off the circuit. Don't be tempted to just flip off the switch that controls the light because the wires at the fixture may be charged even though the switch is off. Make sure none of the wires at the fixture are carrying a charge by testing the bare ends with a voltage tester.

A multifaceted light fixture is an easy and inexpensive way to add sparkle to a kitchen.

1 Remove the existing fixture by unscrewing the nut that holds the glass diffuser or globe in place, then unscrew the nut or nuts that secure the old fixture to the mounting plate.

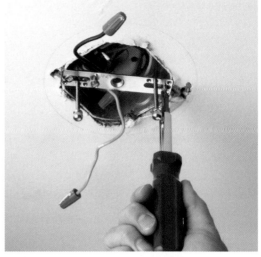

2 Support the loose fixture with one hand, and with the other unscrew the wire nuts connecting the fixture wires to the electrical-box wires. Then separate the wires and remove the old fixture.

3 Remove the old mounting plate and follow the manufacturer's directions for attaching the new mounting plate to the electrical box. If your new fixture is much heavier than the old one, you may have to replace the existing electrical box with a heavy-duty version that attaches between the ceiling joists to support the load.

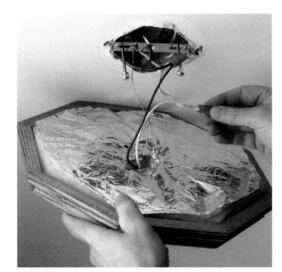

4 Check the manufacturer's directions to see if any assembly is required for your new fixture. When the fixture is ready, just connect the white fixture wire to the white wire from the box and the black fixture wire to the black wire from the box, using wire nuts. Then connect the ground wire from the fixture to the ground wire from the box or to the grounding lug on the mounting plate.

5 Carefully tuck the wiring back inside the electrical box and secure the fixture to the mounting plate with the hardware provided. After adding bulbs and attaching the diffuser, restore power and test the fixture for proper operation.

adding task lighting

An undercabinet strip fixture sheds light right where it's needed.

IN OLDER KITCHENS, MOST OF THE light comes from a single overhead fixture, supplemented by daylight from one or more windows. However, the strength of natural light is subject to the vagaries of time of day, sun exposure, season, and weather. As a result, lighting is often scant when and where you really need it—particularly on countertops. The way to solve this problem is to mount lighting to the underside of overhead cabinets.

Undercabinet lighting is available in a couple of varieties: fluorescent or halogen strips and individual "puck"-style halogen fixtures (see below). Fluorescent fixtures are less expensive than halogen, but halogen provides a light that more closely approximates sunlight. Both types of strips are extremely easy to install and can either plug into a receptacle or be wired to a wall switch.

■ "PUCK" LIGHTS

Some undercounter areas may not need an entire strip of lights. In such cases, small, individual puck-shaped halogen lights are ideal. Puck lights are available in packs of two or more and can be mounted exactly where you need them, then easily wired together with the snap-together fittings provided in the kit. The last puck in the string is connected to a low-voltage transformer, which is plugged into a nearby receptacle.

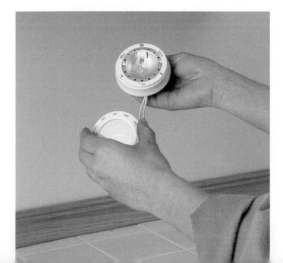

1 If your upper cabinets are wide or your base cabinets are narrow, plug in and turn on the light strip, then move it around under the cabinet to determine its best location. Most undercabinet-light manufacturers recommend installing a strip as close to the front of the cabinet as possible for optimal coverage of the area below.

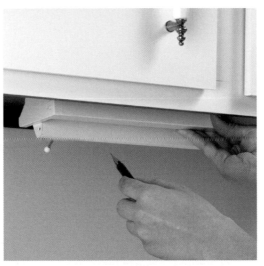

2 Once you've identified the ideal place for the strip, follow the manufacturer's directions for marking the holes for the mounting hardware. Some manufacturers provide a paper template for this; others simply direct you to hold the strip in place and mark though the mounting holes onto the underside of the cabinet.

3 After you've marked the locations for the mounting screws (provided with the light strip), drill pilot holes, then drive the screws into the bottom of the cabinet. Install the strip and plug it in. Fluorescent fixtures can plug right into a receptacle; halogen fixtures usually come with a low-voltage transformer that plugs into a receptacle.

4 Finally, check to see if the light strip is visible at eye level. If it is, make a valance from a ½-inch wood strip 1 to 2 inches wide and the length of the fixture. Finish to match your cabinetry, then glue and nail or screw the valance to the bottom front edge of the cabinet. Not only will a valance hide the fixture, it will prevent glare.

LOWE'S QUICK TIP

Depending on the thickness of your cabinet bottom, you may need to add a washer or two to the mounting screws to prevent them from poking up through the cabinet. Alternatively, you can use shorter screws.

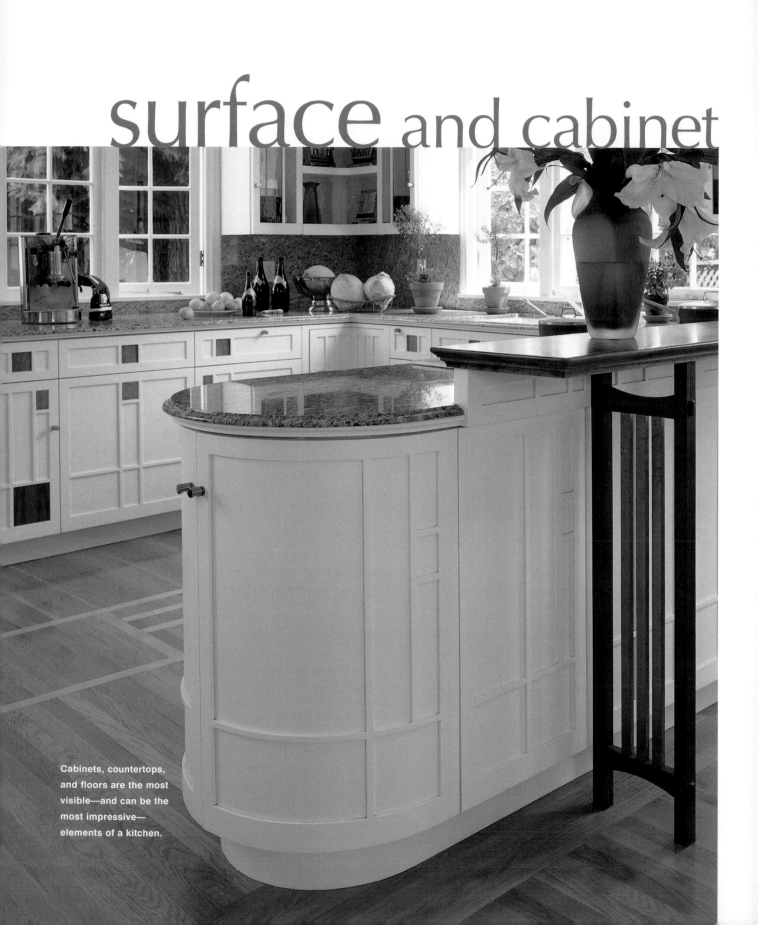

surface and cabinet

Cabinets, countertops, and floors are the most visible—and can be the most impressive—elements of a kitchen.

improvements

ONE REMODELING TASK THAT CAN SAVE YOU REAL MONEY by doing it yourself is making improvements to the kitchen's surfaces: its flooring, countertops, and cabinets. A new floor, freshly tiled counter, and brightly painted cabinets may be all it takes to revitalize a dowdy kitchen. These improvements are also some of the most approachable for do-it-yourselfers, since skills are easily honed as you go, and tool requirements are minimal.

That is not to say these projects don't require a measure of finesse. They demand an eye for detail and a bit of patience—an obsession with measuring and a penchant for perfection are most welcome here. Surfaces are, by their nature, focal points, so slap-dash work will be readily apparent.

The projects presented on the following pages include instructions for laying resilient and ceramic-tile flooring, installing the more demanding prefinished nail-down wood floor, installing and painting cabinetry, and tiling a countertop. If you are a true novice, you might want to start with inexpensive, easily installed materials such as resilient flooring.

One benefit of all these projects is that they are best done with more than one person. Cabinet installation, in fact, demands a helper. If you have a companion with whom you work well, working in tandem will help speed the job along, will give you a second critical eye to evaluate the quality of the work as it proceeds, and will create some pleasant memories to go along with your beautiful new kitchen.

A paintbrush and a notched trowel come in handy for surface improvements.

INSTALLING RESILIENT FLOORING 200

LAYING A TILE FLOOR 202

LAYING A WOOD FLOOR 206

INSTALLING CABINETS 210

TILING A COUNTERTOP 214

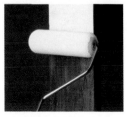

PAINTING CABINETS 218

installing resilient

IN THE WORLD OF FLOORING PRODUCTS, resilient vinyl or composition tile is one of the easier materials to install. The substrate must be clean, flat, and very smooth. A plywood subfloor or an older vinyl floor that meets these requirements will serve. Tiles are uniform in size—normally 12 inches square—and fit together snugly without grout lines. They can be cut with a utility knife and a straightedge. Some tiles have self-adhesive backs, but these tiles tend to be thinner, more limited in selection, and may not form as sure a bond as the types you set with an adhesive compound. Complete instructions for installing self-adhesive tiles come with the tiles. The following directions discuss methods for installing the type applied with an adhesive.

Before you begin, remove everything from the floor and pry off the shoe molding along the base of walls; remove baseboards only if there isn't any base molding. If you'll be covering over old resilient flooring, glue down any loose corners or edges. Flatten embossed flooring and any dips or bumps by troweling on an embossing leveler, then sanding it.

If your floor is very irregular, apply plywood flooring underlayment, made for this purpose, over the top. The edges of these panels interlock; if you must cut perimeter panels, run the cut plywood edges along the walls. Stagger corners so

1 Using a notched trowel held at a 45-degree angle, spread adhesive over the substrate (plywood flooring underlayment is shown here) with long, sweeping strokes that overlap by about 1 inch. Trowel away any excess immediately.

2 When you've waited the proper amount of time, usually about half an hour, carefully position the first tile at the intersection of the working lines. Be sure you get this one right because all the others will be aligned to it.

3 Continue installing more tiles, aligning each tile's edge with a working line or adjacent tile. Let the tiles fall into place rather than sliding them into place or you'll force adhesive up between them. Check alignment and make adjustments every couple of tiles. Clean away excess adhesive as you work and occasionally seat the tiles with a rolling pin or by walking on them.

flooring

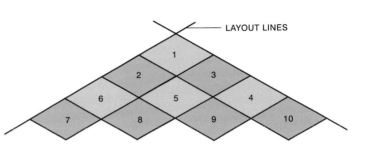

LAYOUT LINES

that four pieces don't come together in one place. Note that plywood underlayment is marked with small crosses; drive a screw or pneumatically shoot a flooring staple at every cross mark. Set the heads of all fasteners below the surface.

If you are applying resilient tile directly over a concrete slab, first fill any holes with floor patch and use a grinder to flatten high spots. Then use a concrete cleaner to prepare the surface for the adhesive.

You can walk on the tiles immediately after installing them, but you can't step on the adhesive, so plan your installation accordingly. Do a dry run first, beginning either at the center of the room or at one wall. If you're tiling from the center, lay

out working lines that intersect at a right angle in the middle of the room (see the illustration above). Use this method if the room is out of square or if you've chosen tile with a pattern or design. Start at the wall only if two adjoining straight walls meet at an exact 90-degree angle.

Follow both the tile and adhesive manufacturers' directions, and note the time it takes the adhesive to dry. Apply evenly and sparingly with a notched trowel (see the adhesive directions for the proper notch size). Allow the adhesive to become translucent and tacky, but not dry, before installing the tiles. Use soapy water or mineral spirits (depending on the type of adhesive) to clean up excess as you work.

Establish perpendicular working lines across the center of the floor. Begin at the intersection of the two working lines and install tiles in the order shown, working toward the edges so that tiles around the border will be equal in size.

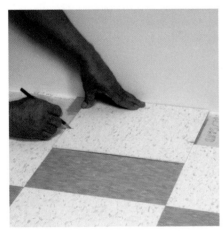

4 To mark a border tile for a straight cut, turn the tile upside down in the correct direction over its future location and press against a ¼-inch spacer at the wall; be sure to keep the tile from touching the adhesive. With a pencil, mark both sides for the cut. Score a single line with a straightedge between the two marks, then hold both sides of the tile firmly and bend it until it snaps.

5 Cut tiles to fit around pipes, doorjambs, and the like. To fit tile around doorjambs, cut a pattern from cardboard, using a contour gauge or compass to transfer the pattern onto a tile. Irregular cuts can be made with a sharp utility knife, scissors, or tin snips if the tile is pliable or can be made so by a hair dryer. If necessary, cut out a piece and glue it in place separately, as shown. Caulk around pipes and cover with a flange.

LOWE'S SAFETY TIP

Resilient flooring installed before 1986 may contain asbestos, which can be a serious health hazard if the fibers are released into the air. Experts recommend either removal by a specialist or covering the old floor with plywood underlayment, then installing the new flooring on top.

laying a tile floor

OF THE VARIOUS FLOORING MATERIALS, ceramic tile is one of the more difficult to install. On the flip side, however, when the job is done, the results are usually well worth the effort. The methods shown on these pages are for laying tile in a thinset mortar base, the method recommended by most professional tile setters (tile can also be installed with adhesive).

preparing a base
Ceramic tile must be laid on a firm, solid, flat base. Several types of existing floors can provide such a base, including concrete slab and wood or plywood subflooring. But a wood or plywood base must be strong enough not to flex when you jump on it. To this end, a plywood or solid-wood subfloor is typically covered with ½-inch tile backerboard or ½-inch plywood underlayment (over the subfloor) as a substrate for ceramic tile. The combined thickness of subfloor and underlayment should be at least 1¼ inches.

Wood strip and plank flooring are not smooth enough to serve as a backing for ceramic tile; cover them with ½-inch plywood underlayment. Similarly, cushioned resilient flooring is too springy to serve as a base, so it should be removed or covered with plywood underlayment, as should badly damaged flooring. Note: Your old resilient floor may contain asbestos; refer to the safety information in the Lowe's Quick Tip on page 201.

New ceramic tile can be applied over

INSTALLING BACKERBOARD

1 Lay down the sheet to be cut. Measure for the cut; subtract ¼ inch for the rough edge. Cut the panel with a cement-backerboard knife, guiding the blade along a drywall square, as shown.

2 Turn the sheet upside down and, holding the board down on one side of the scored line, snap the other side upward. Pick the sheet up on its side, score the back of the cut, and snap the piece back again to free the cut piece. Smooth the rough edge with a tile stone.

3 Sweep the floor free of debris, mix thinset mortar according to label directions, and spread the mortar on the floor using a ¼-inch square-notched trowel. Lay the sheet in the mortar carefully. Drive screws through the sheet into the joists every 6 inches (or as recommended by the manufacturer).

old tile that is in good condition. To improve adhesion of the thinset, roughen the old tile's surface with an abrasive disk mounted in an electric drill (wear a dust mask), then clean the surface with a commercial degreasing agent.

Gently pry up the quarter-round shoe molding along the base of walls before putting in the new floor. Baseboards do not need to be removed unless there is no shoe molding. As you remove the molding, number the pieces with a pencil so you can easily replace them later.

installing **backerboard**

Stagger the joints between sheets of backerboard or underlayment so they don't fall directly over joints in the sub-flooring below, and stagger corners so that four pieces don't come together in one place. If using plywood, interlock the edges; leave a ⅛-inch space between the panels if you're using backerboard. Allow a ¼-inch gap between plywood or backerboard panels and the wall or baseboard. Drive a screw or pneumatically shoot a flooring staple at every cross mark on plywood underlayment. Fasten backerboard

with special backerboard screws, setting all of the screw's heads below the surface.

layout **tips**

You can begin either from perpendicular working lines at the center of the room or along one wall. Begin at the center if the room is badly out of square or if you've chosen tile with a pattern or design. You'll have to cut tiles along all four walls, but the cut tiles will be of equal size. Start at one wall only if adjoining walls meet at an exact 90-degree angle. Then you'll only have to cut tile on two walls. Plan your tiling so you will never have to step on recently laid tiles—this may mean starting at the far end of the room and working toward the door.

Once you've settled on a layout, it's time to establish the working lines that you'll use as guides for the first tiles you lay, as shown above. Butt the first row of tiles up to a batten that's fastened along one of the lines. Once the mortar starts to harden, remove the batten.

cutting **tile**

Mark a cutting line using a pencil or a felt-tipped marker. For 90-degree marks, use a combination square. Angles can be transferred from a wall to a tile with an adjustable T-bevel, and irregular shapes can be transferred with a contour gauge.

Always wear eye protection when cutting. Cut straight lines using a snap cutter or, if you have a lot of cutting to do, consider renting a wet saw with a diamond

Snap two perpendicular chalk lines where you want to begin. Then, to ensure that your first line of tiles will be straight, temporarily screw a batten, or a long, straight board, next to a working line.

4 Lay fiberglass mesh tape over the joints and, using the flat edge of a trowel, spread a thin layer of thinset mortar over the tape. Feather out on either side, and smooth away any high spots. After the thinset is hard, the surface is ready to tile.

NIBBLING AND MAKING CUTOUTS
Nibbling cuts, though not crisp and precise, are accurate enough for most purposes. First score the lines using a snap cutter or a glass cutter, then use a nibbling tool to take small bites out of the cutout area. (Big bites can shatter tile.) Smooth cut edges with a tile stone.

USING A SNAP CUTTER
Position the tile firmly against the cutter's front guide. Lift the handle, and push or pull to score a single, continuous line all the way across the tile. Allowing the cutter's wings to rest on either side of the scored line, push down on the handle; the tile will snap in two. Brush away the debris. For a series of same-sized cuts, position the first tile for a cut and clamp the cutting fence against it—then just hold the next tiles against the fence when cutting.

blade—you'll find it well worth the relatively small expense. Stone, terra-cotta, cement-body, and some porcelain tiles should be cut only with a wet saw. Cut curves or small cutouts with a nibbling tool. For interior cuts, first drill a hole using a masonry bit, then enlarge the hole with a rod saw (this can also be used for cutting curves).

installation tips

Before beginning, open all tile boxes to check for uniform color. If the tile is dusty, wash and dry it before beginning because dust keeps the adhesive from forming a strong bond.

Pay attention to the mortar's open time (the duration of time it remains workable) so you don't end up racing to set the tile before it dries. Once the mortar begins to harden, adjusting tiles is almost impossible. Make a dry run before you begin setting tiles in thinset. The dry run will keep the number of cut tiles to a minimum and prepare you for the unexpected.

For most tile, use gray thinset mortar with a liquid latex additive. For glass tile, marble, or other tile that is translucent, use white thinset mortar. Check with your dealer for the proper mortar. Mix only as much as you can use in about 30 minutes (less if the weather is dry and warm). Be sure to follow label directions. The mortar should be wet enough to pour, and just thick enough to stick to a trowel for a second or two when held upside down.

Maintain properly sized grout joints by using tile spacers; remove them when the mortar begins to set. About every 10 minutes, pick up a tile that you've just set; mortar should adhere to the entire surface. If it doesn't, scrape the mortar off the floor and reset the tile with new mortar. After installing all the tiles, remove the spacers, finish cleaning up excess mortar, and allow to set up for at least 12 hours before walking on the floor.

Prepare grout by adding water sparingly to dry powdered grout, mixing a small quantity at a time. Be sure all particles are

CUTTING WITH A WET SAW
A wet saw typically has a rotating diamond blade that is submerged or drenched with water from a pump (it must be under water when cutting or it will become dull). Slide the tray all the way back toward you and position the tile, pressing it firmly against the guide. Turn on the saw. Holding the tile firmly in place, slide it gently forward against the blade to cut.

laying a tile floor

thoroughly moistened and there are no lumps. For areas of the floor that will be exposed to water, mix in a liquid grout sealer. Always wear rubber gloves when mixing grout, as the lime in it is caustic.

Let the grout cure for the time specified by the manufacturer. Then, if you've used a cement-based grout and the floor is likely to be subjected to standing water, apply a grout sealer for extra protection, following the manufacturer's instructions. Wipe any sealer off the tiles before it hardens. Un-glazed tile (except porcelain) should also be sealed. Use a sealer intended for tile and follow the manufacturer's instructions for applying it.

LAYING A TILE FLOOR

1 Using the smooth edge of a notched trowel, spread mortar on the floor, next to a batten. Then comb the area with the notched edge, holding the trowel at a consistent angle, as shown. Use sweeping strokes to create an even bed.

2 Align the first tile with the working lines, and set into place so you don't have to slide the tile more than about an inch. Then set several more, inserting spacers at every corner. Avoid pressing down when placing tiles.

3 When you finish a section of floor, bed the tiles by setting a short block over two or more tiles and tapping with a rubber mallet. Periodically sight across the tiles to make sure they're forming a flat, level plane.

4 To mark a border tile for a straight cut, place against the wall a spacer that's equal in thickness to the grout lines. Set the border tile on top of the adjacent whole tile and precisely align their edges on all four sides. Set another whole tile on top, then slide the top tile against the spacer. Use the top tile to draw the cutting line across the border tile.

5 Pour about 1 cup of grout onto the floor at a time. Holding a laminated grout float nearly flat, use sweeping back-and-forth strokes in two or more directions to force the grout into the joints. Then tip the float up and, using it like a squeegee, clear away most of the grout by dragging the float diagonally across the tiles. Don't allow its edge to dig into the grout lines.

6 Before the grout dries, wipe the tiles with a large damp sponge (rinse frequently), using light pressure and a circular motion. Smooth and level the grout joints with the tiles. Let the grout dry until a haze appears on the tiles, then polish the tiles with a soft cloth. Apply a grout sealer after waiting the period specified by the grout manufacturer.

laying a wood floor

Beauty isn't skin deep with this hardwood flooring—it's made from environmentally responsible, fast-growing bamboo.

WHEN IT COMES TO WARMTH AND natural beauty, few flooring materials compare with wood. Traditional wood flooring is milled in long strips or planks that are fastened to subflooring. Some types are meant to be sanded and finished; others are prefinished. Unless you're experienced in sanding and finishing wood floors, opt for the latter type—sanding is incredibly dusty work, and a drum sander, in the hands of an amateur, can leave visible ridges and marks.

choosing the **proper base**
New flooring should be installed on a clean, smooth, level, structurally sound base. Depending on the situation and type of new flooring, this base may be an earlier floor covering, an existing wood floor that's in good condition, a new plywood subfloor, or even a moisture-proofed concrete slab (however, preparing a slab should be left to professionals). Following are a few basics for preparing a proper base over a conventional floor.

There are certain advantages to installing wood over an existing floor—you bypass the messy job of removing the old flooring and you gain soundproofing and insulation from the old floor.

One disadvantage to leaving old flooring in place is that you must correct any irregularities in it. Also, the new floor may raise the floor level enough that under-counter appliances (a dishwasher, in particular) won't fit. On the other hand, if you don't put new flooring under the

1 To help prevent squeaks and provide a moisture barrier, cover the subfloor with a layer of 15-pound asphalt felt, overlapping the seams about 3 inches. Tack it down with a staple gun. Measure the room's width at two or more points to establish an accurate centerline, and snap a chalk line to mark it (this line should be parallel to your starting wall). Working from the joist marks along the walls, snap lines to mark the support members.

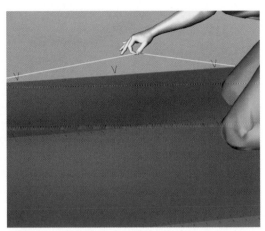

2 Snap another chalk line about ½ inch from the starting wall exactly parallel to your centerline. This is where you'll place the first row of flooring. It will allow a ½-inch gap between the flooring and the wall for the wood's expansion in moist conditions and will be covered by base molding.

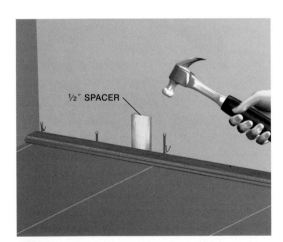

½" SPACER

3 Choose the longest boards or widest planks for the first row. Drill pilot holes for 1½-inch finishing nails, then face-nail the first row through the plywood subflooring to joists or sleepers where the nailheads will be covered by a base shoe. Use a nailset to recess nails below the surface.

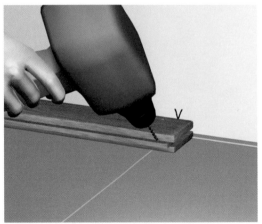

4 On this and the next two rows, blind-nail by hand. First, drill pilot holes at a 45- to 50-degree angle through the tongues, centered on each joist or sleeper at the ends and every 10 inches along the lengths. Fasten with 1½-inch finishing nails. Be very careful not to damage the wood when nailing (use a nailset to finish driving each nail).

laying a wood floor

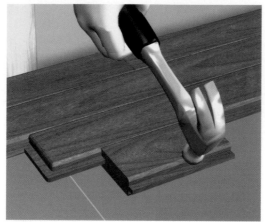

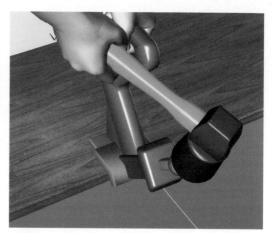

5 Starting with the second row and every row thereafter, move a short piece of flooring along the edge and give it a sharp rap with a mallet to tighten the new row against the previous row before nailing. Avoid having two adjacent joints line up on a joist or over a joint in the subfloor. If you're installing a wide-plank floor where humidity is high, some manufacturers recommend leaving a crack the width of a putty-knife blade between planks for expansion.

6 After the first three rows, continue the nailing with a pneumatic nailer. Slip it onto the tongue and, using a heavy rubber mallet, strike the plunger to drive 2-inch nails or staples through the tongue into each joist or sleeper and midway between them. Be very careful to avoid scratching or damaging the flooring.

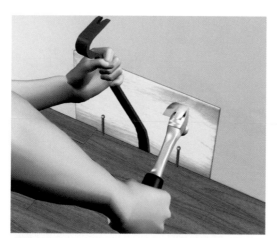

7 Install the final row. Using a block and a pry bar, wedge the final row tightly into position before nailing. Drill holes and face-nail boards where base molding will cover, using the reference lines along the wall to locate the joists. Set the nailheads below the surface, using a nailset.

8 If your new floor will cause a change of level from one room to the next, install a reducer strip for a smooth transition. A reducer strip is milled with a rounded or beveled top. It fits onto the tongue of an adjacent board or, if laid perpendicular to the flooring pattern, onto the tongues at the board ends. It can also be butted against grooves' edges or ends. Face-nail the reducer strip at the floor's edge, set the nailheads below the surface, and fill with wood putty. Last, reinstall the base trim.

appliances, you may not be able to remove them in the future.

Begin by removing all doors, grates, and shoe or base molding. Number the pieces so you can easily replace them when you're finished. If you're going to remove the old flooring, also do that now.

To install subflooring over joists, center the long edges of ¾-inch exterior-grade plywood with a tongue-and-groove edge on the joists. With 2-inch cement-coated or ring-shank nails, nail every 6 inches along the long edges and every 12 inches along intermediate joists. Stagger panels so joints at their ends don't line up over the same joists. For expansion, leave ⅛ inch between panels and ½ inch next to walls (where molding will cover the gap).

laying strip or plank flooring

Before installing wood flooring, give the wood time to adjust to the room's humidity level by leaving it stacked in the kitchen for a few days. With tongue-and-groove plank flooring, decorative screws and plugs can be added after the planks are blind-nailed.

Install the flooring perpendicular to floor joists. With base moldings removed, mark the positions of joists along the wall near the floor for reference. If the room is seriously out of square, position the tongue of the first row of flooring parallel to the centerline and rip the groove side at an angle that will align with the wall.

During installation, it's helpful to lay out several rows of boards, staggering end joints so no end joint is closer than 6 inches to a joint in the next row. As you install the strips, cut pieces to fit at the end of each row (end pieces should be at least 8 inches long), leaving a ½-inch gap between each end piece and the wall.

Cut boards using a radial-arm or power miter saw. When blind-nailing with a hammer and finishing nails, don't try to drive nails flush with your hammer—the indentations will show. Instead, leave each nailhead projecting about ⅛ inch; then

place a nailset sideways over it along the upper edge of the tongue. Drive the nail home by tapping the nailset with your hammer. Then, with the tip of the nailset, set the nail flush with the wood.

"FLOATING" LAMINATE FLOORS

Laminate flooring, a European import now widely popular in the United States, can mimic the look of traditional wood floors as well as tile, stone, and other materials. The surface of laminate flooring is a highly detailed photographic image overlaid with transparent, extremely durable plastic laminate (similar to the countertop material). The base material is a wood-composite product, often medium-density fiberboard (MDF). A backing layer is added to prevent moisture seepage, which can damage the planks.

Laminate floors are installed as floating floors, which means they are not secured to the subfloor. Instead, the individual tongue and groove planks—typically about ⅜ inch thick—are fastened to each other with an adhesive. Some types are installed over a thin foam pad. Special care must be taken when installing laminate floors in kitchens and baths to prevent moisture from seeping between or below the planks. Laminates can be installed over existing flooring materials, including wood, tile, and vinyl; carpeting must be removed. Each manufacturer of laminate flooring products offers complete installation instructions.

installing cabinets

NEW CABINETS CAN MAKE A DRAMATIC difference in the look and feel of a kitchen. Although installing cabinetry does not require professional skills, it does take an eye for precision. In order for cabinets to work properly and look right, they must be installed level, plumb, and flush with each other.

Plan to put in cabinets after rough wiring and plumbing are installed but before you install finish flooring. This way, you won't use more flooring material than necessary and you won't be in danger of damaging new floors. Install wall-mounted cabinets first so the base cabinets won't be in your way as you work.

If your cabinets don't arrive assembled, put them together according to the manufacturer's directions—but remove (or don't install) doors, shelves, and drawers. If you remove these parts, label them so you will know where they go.

The wall behind the cabinets should be smooth, level, and clean. Make sure it's flat by placing a long straightedge against it. Mark any bumpy or bulging areas. During installation, tap wood shims— short pieces of wood shingles—beneath or behind the cabinets to make slight adjustments. If the irregularities are significant, you can compensate for them by using a scribe rail (see the Lowe's Quick Tip opposite).

Upper cabinets are extremely heavy when they're loaded with canned foods or dinnerware, so they must be fastened very securely to wall studs. Screw through a strong part of the cabinet—most have a support rail that runs across the back for this. For each cabinet, at least three screws should penetrate the wall studs by at least 1½ inches.

It is particularly important to install the first wall and base cabinets level and plumb, both from side to side and from front to back, because each additional cabinet will be aligned with the first ones.

European-style frameless laminate cabinets give this kitchen fresh, contemporary styling.

1 Use a level and a pencil to draw a perfectly parallel line across the wall about 3 inches up from the floor. Measure down from this line to the floor to find the floor's high point (if it has one), and mark a line at that point. From there, measure up 34½ inches and draw a level line across the wall to designate the top of the base cabinets.

2 From the 34½-inch line, measure up another 19½ inches and mark a level line across the wall to indicate the bottom of the wall cabinets. Lightly mark the cabinets' dimensions and placement on the wall to double-check your layout.

3 Use a stud finder to locate the wall studs, then, with a pencil, mark their locations above and at least 6 inches below the mark you've made for the bottom of the wall cabinets. Draw straight vertical lines between the top and bottom marks to indicate the center of the studs.

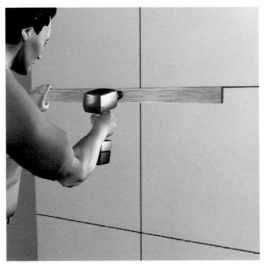

4 Screw a temporary 1-by-3 support rail to the wall, aligning the top edge of the rail with the line for the bottom edge of the wall cabinets. Attach it by driving three or four 2-inch screws through the rail into the wall studs.

LOWE'S QUICK TIP
A scribe rail is a length of wood cut and shaped to fit as a buffer between the wall and the cabinet. You can use a simple compass to trace the wall's irregular surface onto the scribe rail, then trim to ensure a tight fit.

installing cabinets

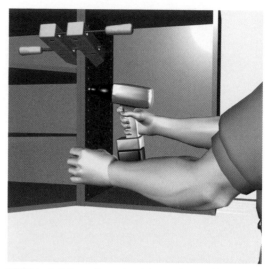

5 Install the corner wall cabinet first, with a helper. Drill pilot holes through the sturdy cabinet back or its support rail and into wall studs. Screw the cabinet to the wall using two screws that are long enough to penetrate the studs by at least 1½ inches, then check the top for level and the front edge for plumb. To correct the position, back off the screws, tap shims behind the cabinet at stud locations, then drive the screws home and add several more into each stud for secure attachment.

6 Install the adjacent cabinets. As you install each one, secure it to its neighbor with a clamp and check it for plumb. On faceframe cabinets, it's easiest to drill two ⅛-inch pilot holes through the sides of the faceframe and use screws. With frameless cabinets, drill bolt holes through shelf-peg holes, then bolt the two together. Be sure not to fasten through shelf-peg holes that you will need for shelves.

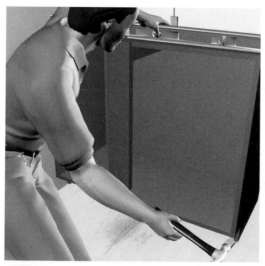

7 After all the wall cabinets are in place, install the corner or end base cabinet. If necessary, use shims to level it and raise it up to the high point of the floor, so its upper edge aligns with the line on the wall. Be sure it is level from front to back and from side to side, then screw it to the wall studs.

8 To turn a corner with base cabinets, push the adjoining cabinet in place and clamp the two units together. Add a filler strip if needed to allow doors and drawers clearance. If necessary, tap shims under the cabinet and behind it to adjust for plumb and level.

updating cabinets

Sometimes all your cabinets need to give your kitchen a whole new look is a bit of basic repair or a few minor improvements. Changing your pulls, for example, can completely alter the look of cabinetry as can refacing (see below) or repainting them (see pages 218–219).

If your cabinet doors droop or shut poorly, repair or change the hinges. First, try tightening the screws. If a screw won't tighten, remove it, squirt a little white glue into the hole and insert some broken-up wooden toothpicks to fill it up (wipe off any excess glue). After the glue dries, cut the toothpicks flush with the surface using a utility knife, and drive the screw into the refurbished hole (you may have to drill a small pilot hole first).

Exposed decorative hinges can also add a new design element to your cabinets. Hinges can be found at Lowe's in virtually every style and size, and in a vast range of materials (see pages 90–91). You're sure to find replacements that will both fit your cabinets and perk up their appearance.

If it seems that your cabinet doors are perpetually hanging open, you may want to switch to self-closing hinges, which do not require a separate catch to keep the door closed.

If you have European frameless-style cabinets and the doors are out of alignment, you may simply need to adjust the hinges. Most of the hinges that attach doors to these types of cabinets can be adjusted with only the turn of a screw to bring the door into line. These hinges are usually mounted directly to the interior cabinet side and are hidden when the door is closed. They do not require a catch since they are self-closing.

Another common, and easily accomplished, repair is adjusting drawers that don't close easily or well. This problem can usually be solved by re-attaching or replacing the drawer's glides.

For the smoothest, most trouble-free drawer opening and closing, purchase prefabricated metal ball-bearing glide sets that attach to the drawer bottom or sides, depending on your drawer's construction and current type of glide. The manufacturer's instructions should detail all you need to know for proper installation.

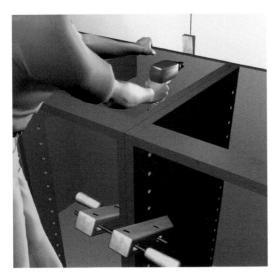

9 Drive screws through the cabinet back (and shims) into the wall studs. Trim any excess material from the shims with a sharp chisel or knife. Continue to add adjoining cabinets in this manner, joining them as you did the wall cabinets in step 6.

REFACING CABINETS

A cost-effective and speedy alternative to completely replacing your cabinets is to reface them. Refacing literally gives a face-lift to your cabinet fronts. With this process, existing doors and drawer fronts are removed and replaced with new ones. Visible surfaces such as cabinet ends and faceframes are finished to match. The cabinet interiors, as a rule, are either refinished or repainted. The results often look as good as if you had replaced the entire cabinet system.

When is refacing, rather than replacing, a good idea? If the basic boxes are in good shape and you are satisfied with your current layout, this could be an attractive option. You can usually choose from a broad range of door and drawer styles, hardware, and finishes.

tiling a countertop

RESISTANT TO HEAT, MOISTURE, AND stains, ceramic tile is an excellent choice for a countertop. If you've never worked with ceramic tile before, tiling a countertop is an ideal first-time project because it's a horizontal and relatively small surface. The keys to a successful tile job are planning and surface preparation.

Before selecting your tile, take careful measurements of your countertop. In calculating the number of tiles required to cover it, be sure to allow for any specialty tiles, such as those needed for edging or a backsplash. (Manufacturers make a number of edge tiles, the most common being the bullnose shown in step 1 on page 216.) To allow for cutting and breakage, order slightly more than you need; the rule of thumb is to buy 10 percent extra. Once you've made your purchase, lay out the tile on the countertop to ensure you have enough for the job and to see where you will need to make cuts.

building a **substrate**

Countertop tiles should rest on a surface that is solid and able to withstand moisture. The front edge must be thick enough to accommodate the edging you have chosen, and the substrate needs to be level in both directions.

In most cases, a layer of ¾-inch plywood topped with ½-inch or ¼-inch cement backerboard will do the job. Although a standard kitchen countertop is 25 inches deep and a backsplash is commonly 4 to 6 inches high, you may want to modify those dimensions slightly in order to minimize cutting of tiles.

Before you begin work, protect the base cabinets from damage and falling mortar by covering them with plastic sheeting or construction paper. Also position a drop cloth on the floor.

Don't forget about the kitchen sink (see pages 102–105 for different types). If you intend to install a flush-mounted sink, do so before the backerboard is in place. If you're planning an undermount sink, install it after the backerboard or after the

1 Attach the plywood to the top of the cabinets by driving 1⅝-inch deck screws (which resist rusting) through the plywood into the cabinet base every 6 inches or so. Cut a hole for the sink following the manufacturer's instructions and make sure the sink fits it. (Attach a flush-mounted sink before adding the backerboard.)

2 Cut backerboard pieces to fit (see pages 202–203). Offset any seams between pieces from plywood seams by at least 3 inches. Lay out pieces in a dry run, and make sure the edges line up precisely with the plywood. Check the sink for fit, as shown. For a flush-mounted sink, bring the backerboard up to the sink edge.

3 Mix a batch of latex-reinforced or epoxy thinset mortar. Spread thinset over the plywood using a ¼-inch notched trowel, spreading only enough for one backerboard piece at a time. Lay the backerboard in the thinset, and drive 1¼-inch backerboard screws in a grid, spaced approximately 6 inches apart.

4 If the backsplash will be tiled with radius bull-nose or quarter-round trim at the top, cut pieces of backerboard to accommodate the thickness and width of the backsplash. Butter the back of the strips with thinset, and press into place against the wall.

5 Apply fiberglass mesh tape to the backerboard joints. Also wrap the front edges of the backerboard and plywood with the tape. Do not apply tape where the backsplash meets the countertop. (Install an undermount sink before tiling.)

For fine-tuning, tile nippers can break off tiny pieces to create curved or complicated profiles. For more about cutting tile, see pages 203–204.

Before you prepare the mortar, place the tiles on the substrate where they will go, with plastic spacers for the grout lines, and make adjustments as needed. Aim for a symmetrical look, with no narrow slivers of cut tiles.

For a countertop that turns a corner, start the layout at the inside corner. If the layout ends with a very narrow sliver, slightly widening the grout lines may solve the problem. In cutting the tiles, take into account the width of the grout lines on either side.

When mixing grout for the installed tile, follow the label instructions. Once the grout becomes firm, wipe off excess with a damp sponge. Allow residual film on the surface to dry to a haze, then buff with a clean, soft cloth. Apply a sealer after waiting the time specified by the manufacturer (typically two to four weeks).

tiling is finished. A typical self-rimming sink is installed after the countertop, as discussed on pages 178–179.

Cut the plywood pieces so they overlap the cabinets by about an inch, and install them with the factory edges facing out. Check the entire surface to make sure it is level as you attach the plywood; if necessary, remove screws, install shims, and re-drive the screws.

Backerboard is easy to cut and install: You simply scribe and snap it, then attach it to the plywood foundation with special galvanized screws. For more about installing backerboard, see pages 202–203. Once backerboard is in place, cover the screw heads with thinset mortar, tape the seams with fiberglass mesh tape, and fill in with thinset mortar.

tiling the **surface**

A tile cutter does an excellent job of scoring and then snapping tile to fit. If the tile is particularly hard, you may need to cut it with a wet saw, which can be rented. When you cut a tile, the result is a sharp edge, which is not only easily damaged but difficult to wipe clean. If possible, position all cut edges at the back of the countertop, where they will be covered by the backsplash tiles.

1 If you're using edging tiles, mark a line along the edge of the countertop to allow for the tiles plus a grout joint, then place a guide strip along this line and temporarily attach it to the countertop with nails. Lay out the field tiles from the edge of the strip to the back of the countertop, using a straightedge to align them.

2 Mix up sufficient thinset mortar for the job and allow it to rest the amount of time specified by the manufacturer. Starting in a corner, apply the mortar to the backerboard with the appropriate-sized notched trowel, working in an area no larger than 2 to 3 square feet.

3 Begin laying tiles by working out from the corner. Press a tile firmly into the mortar, wiggling it slightly as you press down. Continue filling in tiles on either side of the first tile; use plastic spacers to create even gaps for the grout that will be applied later. Once all the full tiles are in place, cut tiles as necessary to fill in. Remove the spacers.

LOWE'S | **QUICK TIP**
Use a fine-point permanent marker to mark cutting lines on tile surfaces.

4 Once all the tiles are set, remove the edging-strip guide and add the edging pieces. The simplest way to do this is by "back buttering"—smear some thinset mortar on the back faces of the edging tile as if buttering a piece of bread. Then position the edging so it butts up against the full tiles, press down, and wiggle to set.

5 Allow the mortar to set up overnight. Then mix up sufficient grout to fill in the gaps between tiles, following the manufacturer's directions. Apply the grout with a grout float held diagonally to the surface, forcing the grout between the tiles. To remove the excess, hold the float at a 45-degree angle and scrape the surface, as shown.

Paint and new cabinet
pulls give these once
dark, outdated cabinets
a new lease on life.

painting cabinets

A FRESH COAT OF PAINT IS A QUICK, inexpensive way to give your kitchen cabinets a new look. Whether you want to lighten up dark and dingy cabinets or liven things up with bold colors, paint provides an instant makeover. Not all cabinets, though, can be painted. Solid wood or wood-veneer cabinets take paint well, as do metal ones; cabinets and faceframes covered with plastic laminate or thinner melamine plastic cannot be painted because paint will not bond properly to these surfaces.

There are three basic tools you can use to paint cabinetry: a brush, a roller, or a spray gun. Brushing paint on large surfaces will leave brush marks; sprayers are expen-

sive and require an enclosure to contain overspray. Rolling is fast, inexpensive, and works exceptionally well on large surfaces; a short (4- or 6-inch) foam roller is a good choice because it lets you cover the face frames with a single stroke and quickly handle the wider doors. As for paint, satin enamel is an excellent choice—it covers well and is easy to clean.

If you're installing new hinges and pulls, make simple drilling jigs to accurately position the hardware. A drilling jig is nothing more than a scrap of ½-inch plywood with holes drilled through it at screw-hole locations, plus strips of wood glued to two adjacent sides for holding it in position (see step 5).

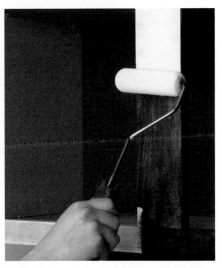

1 Remove all screws, hinges, knobs, and pulls and set aside whichever ones you'll be reusing. Empty the drawers and pull them out. (Although you can try to paint your cabinetry with the doors and drawers in place, in the long run it's a lot easier just to remove them.) Number the doors, drawers, and their hardware to make it easy to replace these properly once you're done painting.

2 Thoroughly clean all surfaces with TSP (tri-sodium phosphate). Rinse completely with fresh water and allow to dry. If you'll be installing new hardware, fill all the mounting holes with putty and allow to dry. Next, sand all surfaces with 150-grit open-coat sandpaper, and vacuum to remove any dust and sanding grit.

3 Mask off all adjacent surfaces and position drop cloths to protect countertops and flooring. Begin by painting the face frames, then turn your attention to the doors and drawers.

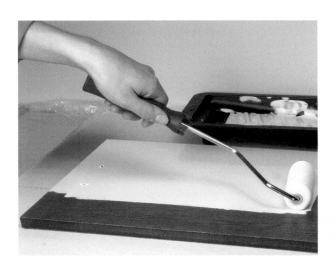

LOWE'S QUICK TIP

Often overlooked, the catches that hold your cabinet doors closed will most likely be worn out and need replacing. Newer magnetic catches are a good choice because they don't wear out.

4 Next, paint the insides of the doors and, while you allow them to dry, paint the drawer fronts. Then paint the fronts of the doors. Depending on the paint you're using, you may or may not need additional coats. If you do, allow the first coat of paint to dry overnight and sand all surfaces with 220-grit wet/dry sandpaper. Vacuum thoroughly and apply the next coat.

5 Once the painted surfaces are dry, install the drawers and attach the doors. Carefully lay out and drill holes through a jig at the desired hardware location. Then position the jig on each door with the strips butted firmly against the door's bottom and side, and drill through the holes in the jig into and through the door. Finally, install the pulls.

credits

DESIGN

PHOTOGRAPHY

index

index

index

Shelving
    budget makeovers and, 26
    entertaining and, 49
    lighting and, 36
    rolling, 88
Shutters, 132–133
Sight lines, 39
Sinks, 102–105
    designing, 14
    installing, 178–179
    islands and, 52
    organization and storage, 65
    space and, 24, 40
    windows and, 36, 39
Skylights, 35, 128, 131
    major remodels, 31
    space and, 39
Space, 22–25, 30, 39–41. *See also* Storage
    family kitchens and, 42
    layouts and, 58
    planning and, 137
Stenciling, 40, 72, 100
Stone
    countertops, 94–95
    flooring, 97
    thresholds, 99
Storage, 64–67, 137. *See also* Space
    accessories, 88–89
    designing and, 69
    islands and, 52
Stoves. *See* Ranges
Subcontractors, 143–147
Subflooring, 200–201, 202, 203, 206, 209.
    See also Flooring
Switches, 127, 192–193

T
Task lighting, 125, 126, 196–197
Thresholds, 99
Tiles.
    See also Ceramic tiles
    cooking and, 97
    countertops and, 94–95, 214–217
    designing and, 14
    flooring, 202–205
    vinyl, 26, 200–201
Tools, 158–161
Track lighting, 124, 126–127.
    See also Lighting

Triangle, kitchen.
    See Kitchen triangle
Trim, 172–175

U
Underlayment, 97, 200–201, 202, 203.
    See also Flooring

V
Valances, 133
Ventilators, 122–123
Views, 35–37
Vinyl
    flooring, 26, 44, 72, 200–201
    tiles, 26
    windows, 128–129

W
Wallpapering, 94, 100–101
Walls, 17, 163–167
Water filters, 107, 110–111
    installing, 186–187
Web sites
    handicap guidelines, 63
    Lowe's, 136, 141
Windows, 128–131
    designing and, 14
    garden, 130
    greenhouse, 39
    major remodels, 31
    style, 17
    treatments, 132–133
    views, 35–37
Wiring, 31, 154–155, 164
    codes, 148
    handicap accessibility, 62–63
    islands and, 52
    receptacles, 190–191
    switches, 192–193
    updating, 189
Wood
    countertops, 94–95
    flooring, 32, 44, 97–99, 206–209
    trim, 172–175
    windows, 129
Work space, 64–67

Z
Zones, 65